13.95

Runner's World

AEROBIC WEIGHT TRAINING BOOK

Runner's World
AEROBIC WEIGHT TRAINING BOOK

**by Ed Sobey
and Gary Burns**

Runner's World Books

Library of Congress Cataloging in Publication Data

Sobey, Edwin J.C., 1948–
  Runner's world aerobic weight training book.
  (Instructional book; 11)

    1. Aerobic exercises. 2. Weight lifting. 3. Phy-
sical fitness. 4. Physical education and training.
5. Sports Training. I. Burns, Gary, 1952–
II. Runner's World. III. Title. IV. Title: Aerobic
weight training book.
RA781.15.S6 1982   613.7'1   82-11315
ISBN 0-89037-230-6 (spiral)
ISBN 0-89037-241-1 (perfect)
ISBN 0-89037-254-3 (hardbound)

Contents

Acknowledgments

The authors gratefully acknowledge the contributions of Sarah Clements, who prepared the graphs, and Frances Wright, who typed the manuscript.

Runner's World Books would like to thank Peter Lehner, an instructor at Los Altos Athletic Club in Los Altos, California, for modeling. Also, thanks go to James Wiltjer, vice president of the Los Altos Athletic Club, for allowing use of the club's facilities. Exercise photos are by *Runner's World* photographer David Keith.

Dedication

To

Woody

and

Scott and Gerald

Preface

This book is a compilation of what we have collectively learned over the past five years of using, teaching and researching aerobic strength training. Although the methods described in this book have been used in whole or part by a number of physical educators and coaches, there has been very little documentation of techniques or results. It is left to the readers to empirically test the methods to deduce what is most useful to their application. This is possible because one of the best features of aerobic strength training is the versatility with which it can be applied. The programs suggested here can be modified to meet the needs of almost any sport or any level of fitness training.

The unifying principles of the diversity of training techniques presented here are those drawn from conventional cardiovascular training and strength training. It is the unique combination of these principles that we call aerobic strength training.

PART ONE
THE BASICS

1

Why Aerobic Strength Training?

The public's perception of fitness and sports training programs seems to have shifted over the years. At one time getting in shape connoted large-muscled men lifting weights. Women were excluded from these programs, because either the training would injure them or the training was a waste of time—after all, women didn't need to be fit.

The recent aerobics boom has changed this view of training. People of both sexes are biking, swimming or running and they form the new image. Century bike rides and 10-kilometer runs are the vogue.

Even more recently the third element of fitness, flexibility, has gained the public's eye. Once the domain of a few eccentrics, yoga and stretching are now advocated by runners and football players alike.

It should be obvious by now that a training mixture of all three elements—strength, cardiovascular conditioning and flexibility—are needed in any serious conditioning or fitness program. That is not to imply that the same training schedule should be pursued by everyone. What it does mean, however, is that a certain amount of training effort must be devoted to each of the three elements in the preparation for any sport. The key question: What is the optimum training mix and how should you go about achieving that desired balance?

This book presents training techniques integrating all three elements. The techniques are flexible enough to fit the training needs of anyone devoted to a particular sport. Understanding the techniques will allow you to devise a program that is uniquely suited to you. We call these techniques aerobic strength training.

The transformation from weightlifting to aerobic strength training occurs by inserting the element of time. In a typical weight-lifting program, rest periods that are long compared to the exercise period are inserted between each set. Although the heart and lungs work heavily during the exercises, there is very little or no aerobic development. By pushing the lifter to maintain a steady and brisk pace for a long duration of exercises, aerobic training occurs. Time is both the motivating force and the control.

The transformation from aerobics to aerobic strength training occurs by using the time-tested principles of strength training. In most aerobic activities, muscles are exercised at low strength levels. Over a long duration these muscles gain strength but they do so at a painstakingly slow pace. The development of the strength needed for aerobic sports can occur much more rapidly and efficiently through the application of strength training principles.

Although not inherently involved in either the strength or aerobic exercises, stretching exercises are an essential element of these programs. Stretching reduces soreness, increases flexibility and speed of movement and lessens the possibility of injury. We recommend that you stretch both before and after aerobic strength training.

There are two fundamental types of programs that we call aerobic strength training. Both use the same training principles and both use the element of time. The way in which they use time, however, is different.

The first method says to do a fixed number of repetitions of each exercise while trying to minimize the time required to finish the workout. This concept is used in outdoor circuit training courses, also known as fitness trails or parcourses. It lends itself to having fixed exercise stations with a distance to be run between each station. It is not recommended in weight rooms, where attempting to run quickly from one station to the next might result in injury.

The second method, applicable in a weight training program, attempts to maximize the number of repetitions of each exercise in a fixed time period. For example, you try to do as many push-ups as you can in a thirty-second interval. This method requires a timer, a person or device, to tell you when to start and stop each exercise.

There are a number of benefits to aerobic strength training programs besides their being able to develop strength and cardiovascular fitness at the same time. These programs can be used by almost anyone, regardless of his level of strength and conditioning. Weights, or the difficulty of the exercise, can be matched to anyone's strength or fitness level. The intensity of the workout can be matched to each person's cardiovascular condition, even when working out with a group where individuals may show a wide range of condition and ability.

Aerobic strength training, particularly utilizing weights, can be adapted to match the specific needs of a particular sport. The strength exercises included, the duration of the workout and the timing for each exercise can be matched to the requirements of almost any sport.

Aerobic strength training can be used for sports training in the off-season or during the season. Like a conventional program, it allows for development of strength during the off-season, but it can also improve endurance before the actual competitive seasons arrive. During the season, workouts once or twice a week can assure strength will be maintained, without harming specific training for the sport.

Aerobic strength training also can be adapted year-round by endurance athletes. Runners who are afraid of bulking up from conventional lifting programs can use aerobic lifting techniques to increase strength and muscle endurance without hindering their running performance.

Another application is in maintaining strength and endurance for athletes who are injured and unable to participate in their regular workouts. Aerobic strength training can maintain cardiovascular endurance and muscle strength and can help to rehabilitate the injury.

A nice feature of these programs is the ability to train large groups of people at the same time. Less confusion occurs than with a disorganized pack of people flooding the weight room. The workouts are highly structured and intense, thereby speeding up workouts considerably. However, they are at the same time flexible enough to allow people with widely divergent goals to work out together.

Groups of up to twenty-five people can easily work out at once, even in a small facility. They need not all do the same exercises, but everyone should know the workout plan so that individuals can assist in changing weight and setting equipment. Weight machines are conducive to this type of training because the weight can be changed simply by moving a pin, eliminating the danger of injury from a falling free weight.

The applications for aerobic strength training are varied. Probably the best application is that of a foundation for a general fitness program. When paired with some other exercise such as running, swimming or biking, which develop high levels of cardiovascular fitness, a commendable general fitness program emerges.

Aerobic strength training, being a mixture of training elements, is a compromise. We believe it to be an ideal compromise, but for those desiring only strength or only cardiovascular conditioning, conventional programs are better. Aerobic strength training does not develop either strength or endurance as quickly as you could with individual, traditional training programs. As you push yourself toward your cardiovascular limits, it is not possible to push simultaneously toward your muscular limits. Thus, strength gains may not be as rapid as possible and may be limited by your state of cardiovascular conditioning. Conversely, the relatively short (fifteen to thirty minutes) workouts are not of sufficient duration to help people interested in developing very great endurance. Recent research indicates that strength gains using an aerobic strength program come closer to the gains expected with conventional programs than cardiovascular improvements. Thus we emphasize including longer endurance workouts with aerobic strength training.

Aerobic strength training is effective and it is fun. People interested in conditioning will enjoy the strenuous, sometimes exhausting workouts. They appreciate that the workouts are short and that they can soon return to the office, home or school after a very time-efficient exercise session. Whether for sports training or fitness, aerobic strength training fills an important niche in an exercise program.

When someone is first confronted with the idea of aerobic strength training, a typical reaction is: "I thought running was the best exercise." Sometimes swimming is used in place of running, or cycling might be suggested. We have no arguments with the proponents of either of these other exercise methods. In fact, throughout this book we suggest that one or more of them can be used to complement aerobic strength training.

We do argue against simple solutions to the problem of keeping your complex body in good shape. Fitness and conditioning have been hampered by the frequent claims of quick, easy or simple-minded plans. An exercise system that requires no work is of no value in conditioning. An exercise system that uses only a few muscles or a few movements of particular muscles is also lacking.

Each exercise system has varying degrees of benefits. We will briefly describe the benefits for four exercises: running, swimming, cycling and aerobic strength training.

In terms of calories-burned-per-minute and aerobic conditioning, running is tops. Running at six-minute-mile-pace consumes fifteen calories per minute and earns 0.75 aerobics points in Dr. Cooper's system. When the pace slows to a slow jog (ten-minute miles), calorie use drops only slightly (to thirteen per minute) but the aerobics value drops sharply (to 0.3 points per minute). If you can run at a moderate pace (eight-minute miles) or faster for several miles, you can be assured of getting a good aerobics workout and burning up many calories.

Running has two drawbacks, however. First, the runner is likely to sustain a series of injuries during his or her running career. These injuries are often painful and usually interrupt the training cycle. Injuries that take several weeks to heal are often discouraging enough to cause the beginning runner to quit. The solution to this problem is injury prevention, through stretching and strengthening, and training within your own abilities. Practicing a second exercise system and having a good mental outlook can be very useful in maintaining conditioning during rehabilitation from a running injury.

The second drawback is that only a few of the skeletal muscles receive a good workout. Most runners recognize the need to supplement their sport with exercises for the stomach, back, knees and, to a lesser degree, arms and shoulders.

Following running in popularity is swimming. Swimming at a good pace (fifty-five yards per minute) almost equals running, in terms of calorie consumption. You burn about fourteen calories per minute. For developing aerobic capacity, however, swimming is not as effective as running (0.45 aerobics points per minute). Swimming exercises more muscles than does running, but unless several kinds of strokes are used, the muscles get exercised in a limited range of motion and not all of the muscle groups are involved. Because swimming does not "overload" the muscles, strength gains occur extremely slowly.

Cycling, even at the moderate pace of thirteen miles per hour, burns up eleven calories per minute, but collects aerobics points slowly (0.1 per minute). Of course, you can probably cycle for more time at a high rate of speed than you can run at a high speed. Thus, as long as you can afford the extra time, you can get as many points cycling as with the other exercises. Increasing your speed will improve the aerobics point production substantially. At seventeen miles per hour, it is 0.28 points per minute. Overuse injuries, which are quite prevalent in running, are less common in cycling. Yet few muscles are used in cycling.

In aerobic strength training you burn calories at the rate of about ten per minute. This is comparable to, but somewhat less than the other exercises. However, you cannot keep up a high level of activity in aerobic strength training as compared to the other exercises. Thus, you will probably burn fewer calories during one workout. At this time we can only make a qualitative statement that says aerobic strength training does develop aerobic capacity. And that rate is slower than for running.

On the positive side, aerobic strength training exercises all of the major muscle groups, and through their full range of motion. Also, unlike with the other exercises, each muscle group can be strengthened progressively and overloaded at optimum training rates. Somewhat surprisingly, injuries occur infrequently.

From this brief comparison, we return to our basic philosophy of exercise. A mix of several systems is much better for overall conditioning than to rely on any one system. Of the four exercise systems discussed, aerobic strength training is the most well-rounded and is the best complement to any of the other systems.

2

Aerobic Training

No other training concept has so captured the attention of this nation of increasingly fitness-conscious individuals as has aerobics.

Since Dr. Kenneth Cooper first detailed the needs and benefits of developing a high level of cardiovascular-respiratory fitness in 1968 and in his subsequent books, millions have jumped on the fitness bandwagon. They have become more knowledgeable about the concepts of their fitness programs and more sophisticated in the use of associated terminology.

It's easy to get caught up—even overwhelmed—by jargon, especially when Joe Neighbor sits before a crowd at the latest party, sipping a club soda with a twist of lime, and explains how his running program contains a mix of 70 percent aerobic workouts and anaerobic interval speed work. He will want to know if you have done any fartlek workouts lately. Later he will argue the merits of isometric and isotonic strength training and will continue all night comparing the benefits of free weights versus Nautilus or similar exercise machines. Before it's over, he will undoubtedly tell you what foods you should be eating.

There is no need to be buried by the ever-increasing volume of terminology and facts of fitness and training methods. Working, not talking, is the only way to achieve your fitness goals. You need learn only some of the basic principles that lay the groundwork for all the programs. If you desire, you can add the more sophisticated techniques and concepts—if and when they suit your training needs.

AEROBICS DEFINED

Although many people use the word aerobics, few have a solid understanding of what it means. Literally, aerobic means in the presence of oxygen. From an exercise standpoint, an aerobic activity is one that promotes sufficient activity of the heart and lungs for sufficient time to create some beneficial changes in the body and in the cardiovascular-respiratory system itself.

Also known as sub-maximal exercise, activities such as running, swimming, dancing, and many others, require a steady flow of oxygen. The cardiovascular system becomes more adept, with training, at handling this flow of oxygen, creating a positive training effect (that is, an improvement in conditioning).

In contrast, anaerobic exercises are those done without a constant flow of oxygen. Muscle activity is supported by energy-releasing reactions that occur without oxygen. Sprinting, lifting weights and other similar activities that are done quickly with little extended breathing are anaerobic. Some exercises, particularly running, can pass from an aerobic exercise to anaerobic, depending on pace changes.

Any exercise requires energy production by both aerobic and anaerobic mechanisms. However, the shorter the exercise duration the larger the percentage of total energy supplied by anaerobics becomes. As the time of exercise increases, the energy contribution of aerobics increases.

Activities that last less than two minutes are largely anaerobic while those that last longer than five to ten minutes are largely aerobic. The anaerobic mechanism supplies energy quickly and is used at the start of an exercise session or when the pace of exercise is increased. Once at a steady, sustainable level of exercise, the aerobic mechanism takes over; however, if the aerobic capacity is exceeded, then the anaerobic mechanisms supplement the aerobic ones.

The anaerobic reactions occur rapidly but have little endurance. Aerobic reactions have endurance but require a few minutes to come up to full speed.

The following chart shows the varying percentages contributed by aerobic and anaerobic mechanisms. It also can give you an idea of the time required for the anaerobic to aerobic transition to occur.

The cardiovascular system, working in conjunction with the lungs, processes this oxygen. When air fills the lungs, it attaches to the hemoglobin in red blood cells, then is pumped through the blood vessels by the heart for use by tissue in various parts of the

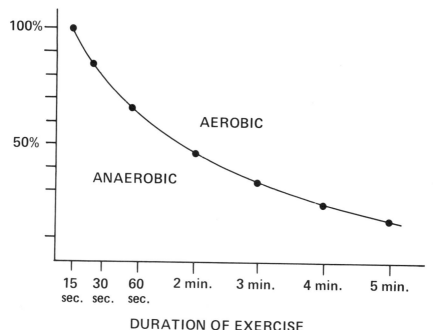

DURATION OF EXERCISE

body.

The demands on the heart are phenomenal and varied. Consider the strength and power of a muscle that is asked to range its work from a 70-beat-per-minute resting rate (on the average) to nearly 200 beats per minute in periods of heavy exercise. Consider also that it's expected to provide trouble-free service for over seventy years, in the average individual. Aerobic exercise is one form of maintenance you can provide to make sure that your heart does keep performing efficiently.

THE TRAINING EFFECTS

The changes produced in the body through aerobic exercise are cumulatively known as the training effect. There are several elements:

1. Aerobic exercise strengthens the muscles of respiration, reduces resistance to air intake through respiratory passages and facilitates the rapid flow of air in and out of the lungs. Studies conducted by David Costill, and other scientists, on distance runners involved in long-term aerobic training have indicated an above-average maximum breathing capacity and an expanded vital capacity. Maximum breathing capacity is the largest volume of air that can be breathed by an individual in one minute. Vital capacity is

the amount of waste gas that can be expelled through the lungs. Increasing both of these measures improves the athlete's ability to perform endurance activities.

2. Aerobic exercise improves the strength of the heart muscle. This means that more blood can be pumped and therefore more oxygen can be carried to the body muscles.

The exercise may also have a compound effect of reducing the heart's overall work. While studies have shown that well-conditioned athletes frequently have very low resting heart rates, the volume of blood being pumped in a single stroke can, by comparison, be as much as twice the average individual's.

3. Aerobic exercise helps tone muscles and improve general circulation. Cardiovascular conditioning has been shown to increase the buildup of blood vessel networks within the exercised muscle groups, because their need for oxygen is greater. Blood vessels also become more flexible through conditioning, which eases blood flow.

4. Aerobic exercise helps increase the efficiency of the lungs. Well-trained individuals utilize more of the upper portions of their lungs, thereby providing more access to oxygen during hard exercise.

All the elements of the aerobic training effect combine to help increase the amount of oxygen that the body is able to process in a given time. That is, they help increase the aerobic capacity.

Scientifically, aerobic capacity is measured through the individual's maximal oxygen uptake (VO_2 max). Active twenty-year-olds may have a capacity of 44 to 47 milliliters of oxygen per kilogram of body weight per minute (44-47 ml/kl/min). Studies on standout distance runners reveal far greater VO_2 max levels and the ability to use a much higher percentage of that aerobic capacity. The late Steve Prefontaine, one of our best middle-distance runners of the past decade, had a VO_2 maximum nearly twice the average.

5. The work of Dr. Ralph Paffenbarger at Stanford University shows that exercise may be a factor in reducing the threat of heart attack and helping to reduce other heart ailments.

Remember, however, that none of these training effects is automatic. If the exercise is not of sufficient length and intensity, no training effects will occur.

GETTING STARTED

In fitness training, as for any other long-range endeavor, you must know not only where you want to go, but also where you're starting from. Fortunately, it's becoming much easier these days to determine the state of your fitness.

Although starting an exercise program—aerobic training, strength training or a combination—is generally not dangerous to your health, if you have any special health problems you should consult your doctor before beginning. This is especially true for those with high coronary risk factors or who have a family history of heart disease.

However, a checkup is a good idea for anyone, particularly if they haven't been exercising or had a physical in a couple of years. People over thirty should have an annual checkup.

One of the most accurate measures of cardiovascular fitness is the stress electrocardiogram (ECG), treadmill test. The important word here is "stress."

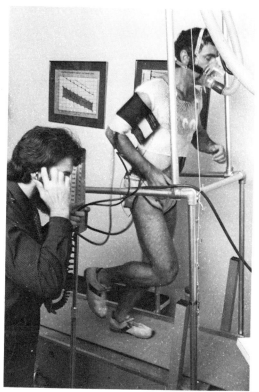

Taking a stress test on a treadmill is one way to find heart problems.

While the ECG by itself is able to monitor and record the heart-beat pattern, irregularities often do not occur until the individual undergoing testing is stressed to a level near his maximum heart rate. These irregularities, which signal potential heart disease, often do not show up during a non-stress ECG. Many university and fitness research facilities now offer such testing, which may include analysis of VO_2 levels, blood tests and a more complete fitness profile.

While the stress test is recommended because it is one of the most accurate testing methods available, it's not the only one. A variety of basic fitness tests can be performed by the individual. These tests are not as complete and do not reveal deep-seated heart abnormalities.

The most basic home test is to record your resting heart rate. Find your pulse with your fingertips (not thumb, which has a strong pulse of its own) just inside your wrist in line with the thumb. Using a very light touch you can check a pulse at the cartoid artery, which runs along either side of your neck. Note that heavy pressure on this artery alters your results.

Count the heartbeat for fifteen seconds, then multiply by four to obtain the resting rate in beats-per-minute. The resting rate varies among individuals, depending on heredity, recent strenuous exercise, level of fitness and other factors, and is not a totally reliable measurement. But, generally, under 52 beats per minute (bpm) indicates a highly conditioned male (58 bpm for women). A reading of 88 bpm or more indicates, to me, poor condition (94 bpm and more for women). The average pulse is approximately 63 - 70 bpm for men and 69 - 76 bpm for women.

To improve the reliability of results, exercise for a set time and measure the time required for your pulse to return to normal. One test that does this is the Harvard Step Test. The procedure calls for stepping up on and then down from an elevated object whose height corretates with yours. During the four-minute test you are to complete thirty steps a minute. Obviously, do not attempt the test if you are in really bad condition.

To maintain the required pace, a metronome helps, or have someone count every two seconds. Do not alternate feet on each step. Step up on one foot for two minutes before switching feet.

After the four minutes (or sooner if you can't complete four minutes), sit quietly for one minute and then count your pulse for thirty seconds, and rest for thirty seconds. Repeat this procedure twice more so that you have taken your pulse at three one-minute intervals. Add those three totals and plug them into this formula.

$$\text{Recovery index score} = \frac{\text{Duration of Exercise (in seconds) x 100}}{\text{Sum of pulse counts x 2}}$$

A guide to your level of conditioning is indicated below.

Recovery Index Score	Condition Level
less than 61	poor
61 - 70	fair
71 - 80	good
81 - 90	very good
over 90	excellent

To compensate for height differences, vary the size of the step as follows:

Your Height	Height of Step
Below 5' 0"	12 inches
5' 0" - 5' 3"	14 inches
5' 3" - 5' 9"	16 inches
5' 9" - 6' 0"	18 inches
over 6' 0"	20 inches

Another method is the Kasch Step Test, performed for three minutes on a twelve-inch step. Perform two *complete* steps every five seconds. When you step up, both feet must touch the top of the step and be straight. Recover with both feet on the ground. The tricky part of this test is to start counting your heart rate just five seconds after you are finished exercising. Count your pulse for a full minute. Use the total to find your fitness level.

TABLE 1

KASCH STEP TEST

	Highly Conditioned	Average	Poor
Males			
20 - 39 years	less than 79	87 - 107	over 119
40 and over	less than 82	90 - 110	over 122

TABLE 1 cont'd.

KASCH STEP TEST

	Highly Conditioned	Average	Poor
Females			
20 - 39 years	less than 83	91 - 111	over 123
40 and over	less than 86	94 - 114	over 126

Perhaps the simplest and most popular test of aerobics is Cooper's twelve-minute running test. Find a track or accurately measured distances along a running route. The test is to see how much ground you can cover, either by running, walking or a combination, in twelve minutes. Use the tables below to determine your aerobic fitness level. The distance units used here are miles.

12-MINUTE TEST
MEN

Condition Rating	Age			
	13 - 19	20 - 29	30 - 39	40 - 49
Very poor	under 1.30	under 1.22	under 1.18	under 1.14
Poor	1.30 - 1.37	1.22 - 1.31	1.18 - 1.30	1.14 - 1.24
Fair	1.38 - 1.56	1.32 - 1.49	1.31 - 1.45	1.25 - 1.39
Good	1.57 - 1.72	1.50 - 1.64	1.46 - 1.56	1.40 - 1.53
Excellent	1.73 - 1.86	1.65 - 1.76	1.57 - 1.69	1.54 - 1.65
Superior	over 1.87	over 1.77	over 1.70	over 1.66

WOMEN

Condition Rating	Age			
	13 - 19	20 - 29	30 - 39	40 - 49
Very poor	under 1.0	under .96	under .94	under .88
Poor	1.00 - 1.18	.96 - 1.11	.95 - 1.05	.88 - .98
Fair	1.19 - 1.29	1.12 - 1.22	1.06 - 1.18	.99 - 1.11
Good	1.30 - 1.43	1.23 - 1.34	1.19 - 1.29	1.12 - 1.24
Excellent	1.44 - 1.51	1.35 - 1.45	1.30 - 1.39	1.25 - 1.34
Superior	over 1.52	over 1.46	over 1.40	over 1.35

From Kenneth Cooper, *The Aerobics Way* (c) 1977

If you place good, or higher, you can begin aerobic strength training at the recommended beginning levels. If you fall into the lower categories, you should first improve your aerobic fitness before trying an aerobic strength program.

MONITORING PROGRESS

Periodic testing of aerobic fitness and keeping a record of gains is incentive enough for some to continue the program. The testing and comparing of test results become the reasons for exercising.

Cooper has devised a simple point system that allows you to evaluate the aerobic benefits from a variety of exercises and sports. After years of research, Cooper contends that thirty aerobics points per week for men, and twenty-four for women, are enough to maintain an adequate level of cardiovascular fitness. You should accumulate the points during at least three different workouts a week. Most serious athletes will readily exceed these minimums.

Here are some examples of an exercise and how many points it scores:

Running a mile in seven minutes earns you five points on the aerobic scale, as would swimming six hundred yards in ten to fifteen minutes or riding your bicycle six miles in twenty-five minutes. See Cooper's book for the complete tables.

The aerobics point system is based on an estimate of the oxygen required to perform an activity beyond your basic, resting needs. One aerobics point is the equivalent of 7 ml/kg/min (milliliters of oxygen per kilogram of body weight per minute). If running a mile costs 42 ml/kg/min, the point value is six (42 ml/kg/min divided by 7ml/kg/min). Cooper has found that, on the average, a person uses 42 ml/kg/min while running a mile in 6:30. Thus, if you run a mile in 6:30 you earn six points.

The charts in Cooper's books are also adjusted for duration and length of activity. They offer more points for extended exercise at the same pace. For those considering an overall aerobic conditioning plan utilizing a variety of activities, the aerobic tables are invaluable.

To measure aerobic training without tallying points all week, consider taking a pulse count after exercise. Since the heart rate or pulse is proportional to the workload imposed on it and on the body's consumption of oxygen, it is a good measure of the total exercise load. Take your pulse at the end of each exercise session and record it. For consistency, count the pulse at a set time after exercise. Because the pulse rate begins to drop as soon as you stop exercising, take a pulse as soon after exercise as is practical. Count beats for a ten- or fifteen-second interval and multiply by six or four to get the number of beats-per-minute. The result is a good comparison of how hard you have worked through the training session. The higher the pusle count, the harder you worked. After monitoring your post-exercise rate for a few weeks, you will learn what pulse range occurs with various levels of workout stress.

Pulse rates vary considerably from one person to the next. In general, for an identical workout, the person with the lowest pulse is in the best cardiovascular condition. However, because of the large differences in individuals' pulse rates, the pulse rate only has value as a personal indicator of conditioning and exercise intensity.

Take your pulse at various times of the day—in the morning before rising, before and after exercising, and while working. After a few days of monitoring your pulse, you will know how it reacts to a variety of stresses. The day after a very hard workout you might find an increase in your heartbeat of ten per minute, indicating you had a tough workout. You should use caution and run an easier workout at the next session.

The heart rate is also an analytical tool that helps you maintain a maximum training effect for each exercise session. The rule of thumb is that for a training effect, your exercise should raise your heart rate to between 70 and 80 percent of your maximum heart rate.

Your theoretical maximum pulse rate (TMPR) is calculated as follows:

$$TMPR = 220 - age$$

For example, if you are thirty years old, your theoretical maximum pulse is 190 beats per minute. To get cardiovascular training, your exercise pulse should be at least 133 beats per minute but no higher than 162 beats per minute. Remember, this is only a rule of thumb; your pulse rate may not conform to this rule. The best guide is your knowledge of your own pulse and how it varies with different exercise.

CARDIOVASCULAR TRAINING TABLE

HEART RATE CHART

Age	Maximum Heart Rate (Beats per minute)	Exercise Heart Range (Beats per minute)
20 and below	200	140 - 170
21	199	139 - 169
22	198	139 - 168
23	197	138 - 168
24	196	137 - 167
25	195	137 - 166
26	194	136 - 165
27	193	135 - 164
28	192	134 - 164
29	191	134 - 163
30	190	133 - 162
31	189	132 - 161
32	188	132 - 160
33	187	131 - 159
34	186	130 - 158
35	185	130 - 157
36	184	129 - 156
37	183	128 - 156
38	182	127 - 155
39	181	127 - 154
40	180	126 - 153
41	179	125 - 152
42	178	125 - 151
43	177	124 - 151
44	176	123 - 150
45	175	123 - 149
46	174	122 - 148
47	173	121 - 147
48	172	120 - 146
49	171	120 - 145
50	170	119 - 145
51	169	118 - 144
52	168	118 - 143
53	167	117 - 142

CARDIOVASCULAR TRAINING TABLE

HEART RATE CHART

Age	Maximum Heart Rate (Beats per minute)	Exercise Heart Range (Beats per minute)
54	166	116 - 141
55	165	116 - 140
56	164	115 - 139
57	163	114 - 139
58	162	113 - 138
59	161	113 - 137
60	160	112 - 136
61	159	111 - 135
62	158	111 - 134
63	157	110 - 134
64	156	109 - 133
65 and above	155	109 - 132

Do not count your pulse for a minute, because the rate will change quickly as you count. Instead, take your pulse by counting for ten or fifteen seconds and multiplying it by either six or four, respectively.

Take your pulse rate several times during the course of an activity to be sure you are maintaining the desired level. This can be important in a prolonged exercise in which your pace may vary, or if you are like so many of us who tend to slack off a little as the workout gets longer and tougher. Monitor the pulse three or four times on a ten-second basis, during the exercise and again at the end. Use those readings to find an average, a more accurate measure of the work performed by your heart during the training session.

APPLICATION

The success of any aerobic program depends principally on three criteria:

1. How often you exercise;

2. How long you exercise;

3. How intensely you exercise.

First, researchers now generally agree that in order to have a positive, long-term effect, exercise must be done at least three days a week on non-consecutive days. Exercise less and you gain little improvement. Over-exercise by not alternating hard workout days with easy days and you will have reduced energy, greater chance of injury and staleness.

Second, ten minutes of cardiovascular exercise a day isn't going to give you much training effect. Most researchers feel you need a minimum of between twenty and thirty minutes a session to improve your cardiovascular fitness.

Third, intensity of the exercise session is measured by using the pulse test at frequent intervals and making sure that the average pulse rate for the exercise stays between 70 and 80 percent of maximum.

In our example, a thirty-year-old could exercise at least three times a week. He should keep his pulse between 133 and 162 beats per minute for at least twenty to thirty minutes per session.

If you find that your pulse rate is below the 70 percent guideline, try working slightly harder. If you feel fine, continue at the higher intensity. Otherwise return to the lower intensity and realize that your normal pulse rate may be lower than the average.

WARMUP, STRETCHING, WARMDOWN

Armed with knowledge of your basic fitness level and ways to periodically measure it, your initial reaction is to charge into a workout. But many people totally ignore two of the most crucial periods of any exercise program--the few minutes before and after exercise.

The warm-up period is the time in which you prepare your mind, muscles and cardiovascular system for the strenuous exercises that follow.

To prepare your mind you should plan, or review your plans for the workout. What do you want to accomplish? How will this workout help you achieve your long-term conditioning or athletic goals? Where, in your previous workout, did you have the most difficulty? How will you overcome that difficulty in this workout?

In strength training you might want to formalize the mental part of the workout by writing a plan in terms of sets, reps and weights. This is especially important for beginners and the experienced who are returning after a layoff.

Planning your workout will help you to select realistic goals. Try to stick to your goals but don't be afraid to change them if you run into trouble. A plan is, after all, only a statement of what you think you will do—it is not a signed contract, with conditions you are obliged to meet.

Mental preparation for a workout includes focusing your attention on the workout. This is a time to forget the stresses of the job, school or whatever. Your workout is the one time of the day you can be selfish and the warmup is your mental transition period to adjust to this.

If you've been sitting all day, your pulse is probably slow. You're not ready to go straight into a heavy workout. Do two to three minutes of easy exercises (jumping jacks, for example) to elevate your pulse and help raise your body temperature. You will have more strength when your body temperature is slightly higher than normal.

Next, stretch slowly. This is the most important element in the warmup. Stretching yields:

1) Increased flexibility — the ability to move through the full range of possible motion.

2) Injury prevention — stretching reduces the possibility of muscle pulls.

3) Prevention of muscle stiffness

4) Relaxation of muscles

5) Increased muscle power — although stretching does not in itself increase strength, it allows for faster muscle contraction and thus greater power.

Stretching should be static, not ballistic or bouncing. In static stretching, a stretch position is held, usually for fifteen to thirty seconds, without moving. Most of us learned ballistic stretching methods, commonly associated with calisthenics. Actually, the bouncing triggers nerve firings that result in muscle contraction. Also, it's easier to overstretch a muscle while doing ballistic stretches than with static stretches.

Hold each stretch at a comfortable position for fifteen to thirty seconds. You should feel the pleasant sensation of stretching, but not pain. If your breathing is irregular, you are probably stretching too far.

The stretch feeling should gradually dissipate as the stretch is held—if not, you're probably over-stretching. If the sensation has significantly decreased by the end of the stretch, slightly increase the amount of stretch. Hold this new position for fifteen to thirty seconds, then relax.

Here are a few basic stretches. We urge you not to forget the importance of stretching in your overall conditioning program.

Groin Stretch — While sitting on the floor, bring the soles of your feet together. Grab your feet with your hands, lower your knees toward the floor and lean forward into the stretch.

Groin Stretch

In the groin stretch, touch your heels together.

Toe Touches

This is the standard toe-touch position.

The crossed-leg toe touch gives more stretch.

Toe Touches — Stand with your feet shoulder-width apart. Lean over and bend until you feel the stretching sensation in your hamstrings. Keep your knees straight. To increase the stretch cross the feet and repeat the procedure. When standing up flex your knees slightly to take the strain off your back muscles.

Legs Over Head — Lie on your back and bring your legs over your head and rest your toes behind your head, on the floor. If you cannot get your toes on the floor, just stretch as far as is comfortable. This stretches the lower legs and back.

Side Bends — From a standing position, bend directly to your side. Make sure you do not arch your back, which strains the back muscles. Alternate sides.

Legs Over Head Stretch

In Legs Over Head, stretch as far as is comfortable.

Side Bends

In the side bend do not arch your back.   Bend directly to your side. Work both sides.

Shoulder Stretch — Put your right hand behind your head, on your left shoulder blade. With the left hand, gently pull your right elbow to the left. Alternate sides.

Achilles and Calf Stretch — Remove your shoes to get a good stretch from these exercises. Start about two to three feet from a wall. Take half a step forward with one foot and rest your arms against the wall. Keep your feet flat on the floor and pointed forward. You will feel the stretch in the calf of the back leg.

From the same position, bend the back knee slightly to move the stretch to the Achilles tendon. Repeat on the opposite leg.

These two stretches are very important for anyone who runs. They should be included in pre- and post-running stretching programs.

Shoulder Stretch

In the Shoulder Stretch, your right hand goes on your left shoulder blade.

Achilles and Calf Stretches

For the Calf Stretch, lean against a wall.

Bend the back knee slightly to move the stretch to the Achilles tendon.

Thigh Stretches — This exercise can be done either while standing or lying down. If done while standing, steady yourself on a wall or post with the opposite hand. Bend one leg at the knee and bring that foot up to your buttocks. Grab the toes with your free hand (on the same side as the bent leg) and pull your toes even closer to the buttocks. Repeat on the other side.

Thigh Stretch

Hold your foot with one hand and lean against a wall with the other in the Thigh Stretch.

Shoulder Hang — Grab a bar or fence about shoulder-height. Stand about three feet away from the fence. Keeping your legs straight and vertical, ease just your chest and head downward and toward the fence.

Body Hang — Grab a chinning bar with an overhand grip. Relax all your muscles—except the grip—and let your body hang.

Door Frame Stretch — With your back toward an open doorway, grab the frame on each side, your hands facing outward. Straighten the arms and lean forward to feel the stretch in shoulders and chest. This is good for improving the posture of those with slumped shoulders.

Hamstring Stretch — Find a bench or fence that is about hip high. Rest the heel of one leg on the bench, standing on the other leg with toes pointed forward. Keep both knees straight. Lean forward at the waist toward your elevated knee until you feel the stretch. Repeat on other leg.

The warmdown is as important as the warmup. A good warmdown helps prevent sore muscles and is the first step in preparing for your next workout.

Muscle soreness is caused by the inefficient removal of wastes in the muscle. If you are just starting a training program or are increasing your training, expect sore muscles for one or two days. Continuing your workouts is the best way to eliminate soreness, because muscles adapt to the increased demands and become more effective at removing the waste products. If you skip a few days to let the soreness go away, it will. But the soreness will return as soon as you start again.

Stretching can help reduce the soreness. Repeat the stretches you did in the warmup. You may notice that you can stretch farther after exercising than before, because the muscles may have loosened up. Remember to stretch to the comfortable limits.

Heat (twenty to thirty minutes at a time) helps relax muscles and increases the blood flow, which will help eliminate wastes. Massage is also helpful.

3

Strength Training

PRINCIPLES

It seems that everyone has a different idea of how to most efficiently gain strength through weight training. But few of the various methods have been adequately tested or compared. In strength training there are only two basic principles that are universally accepted. As long as you adhere to them, you will be successful in gaining strength.

The two principles are the Specificity Principle and the Overload Principle. The specificity principle is also known as the concept of Specific Adaptation to Imposed Demands (SAID). Basically, it says that the body will adapt itself to perform the work that is asked of it. You gain strength by forcing your muscles to work. You improve cardiovascular conditioning by using your cardiovascular system in demanding workouts.

Training must be specific to your sport. If you want to run marathons, it doesn't do any good to spend all your training time doing push-ups or throwing a football in the back yard. Conversely, being able to run 6:30 miles for an hour will not help you hold off an onrushing linebacker long enough to let your quarterback escape or throw the ball. Your program must be designed to develop useful strength that closely approximates the demands and movements required in your sport.

To most effectively design your training routine for a sport, you need to determine what motions will be performed, which muscles will be used, and at what speed and for what duration will the motion be repeated. By considering all of these elements in planning your strength program you can design a more specific workout for your sport.

The range of motion in strength training is crucial. An exercise that follows a limited range of motion will develop strength only through that limited range. Strength gained at one position does not transfer to all positions. A common mistake in strength training is to limit the motion so that you can do more repetitions. You might think that you are getting a better workout that way, but you aren't. To develop strength throughout the entire range of a muscle, you must exercise through the full range. In addition, the muscle must be overloaded throughout its entire range.

Going through the entire range of motion also has the extra benefit of maintaining flexibility. As you exercise muscles they tend to become shorter and tighter if worked only through a short range of motion. Being limited in the range of motion is what we call being muscle-bound.

The specificity principle is also important in determining the speed of exercise movement. Exercise speed should be similar to the movements in the sport or activity in which you intend to use the muscles. Training for a speed event requires fast repetitions of the exercise. Training for an endurance sport requires more repetitions, usually at a slower rate. The exercise resistance, or weights, is adjusted so you can perform the designed number of repetitions.

Strength training affects the three different types of muscle fibers: slow-twitch, fast-twitch and a third, fatigue-resistant fast-twitch groups. Slow-twitch fibers are rich in capillaries. They fatigue slowly and are responsible for the endurance capacity of the muscle. Fast-twitch fibers fatigue quickly but can contract rapidly and can quickly provide a great deal of strength. The third type of fiber, recently discovered, has characteristics of both.

Everybody is born with a certain proportion of fast- and slow-twitch fibers. Training cannot alter that proportion, but it can increase the capacity of one or the other to perform work. World-class distance runners and other endurance athletes have a high percentage of slow-twitch fibers. Sprinters, olympic weightlifters and others who excel at sports requiring sudden bursts of energy, have a greater proportion of fast-twitch fibers. A table shows the distribution of fast- and slow-twitch fibers in the muscles of various athletes.

Sport	Percentage	
	Fast-Twitch	Slow-Twitch
Olympic weightlifters	83	17
Sprinters	78	22
Downhill skiers	52	48
Marathoners	26	74

Source — *Endurance Training for the Elite Runner*, Pat O'Shea.

For your strength training to be most effective you must plan it toward developing the muscle fibers that will be used in your sport. If you are training for a marathon, think endurance and build the slow-twitch fibers.

The second principle, the overload principle, is simple enough. To become stronger, a muscle must be overloaded—subjected to more work than it is used to. As training continues and the muscles strengthen, the weight or exercise resistance must be increased so that it is larger than what the muscle has adapted to. Using a lighter weight or smaller resistance will result in only minimal, if any, strength gains. This point is dramatically illustrated in the following figure. The two curves represent two test groups, and their

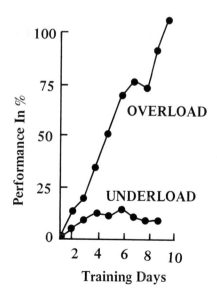

Reprinted from *Physical Therapy* (Vol. 36: pp 371 - 383, 1956) with the permission of the American Physical Therapy Association.

strength improvement in an experiment on exercise techniques.

The group represented in the upper curve used weights that over-loaded their muscles. The group on the lower curve used lighter weights. Each did an equivalent amount of work in training. The group with lighter weights did more repetitions. The work load is defined as the product of weight, repetition and distance moved. Although the second group used lighter weights, their work out-put was the same as the first group because they had more repetitions.

The difference is obvious. The underloaded group experienced little strength improvement, while those overloading their muscles had large strength gains.

Consider the applications of the overload principle in sports. Distance runners do not overload their upper bodies while running. Arms, neck or back may get tired, but never any stronger. There-fore, progressive exercise to strengthen upper body muscles and prevent fatigue is necessary.

To effectively overload a muscle, you must first isolate it. That is, you must design and use an exercise for only a particular mus-cle to perform—one for which other muscles cannot assist. For example, if you do chin-ups with your feet on the ground you will tend to use your leg muscles to push yourself upward.

Isolating the muscles to be exercised isn't always easy, though. In almost any action, the contractions of many muscles are re-quired. The larger muscles of a set will end up doing most of the work. This makes it difficult to strengthen the smaller muscles. If they are not isolated, the larger muscles will do the work but may not be overloaded—thus, the exercise accomplishes little.

Consider the isolation concept in the standing press. While the exercise is designed to strengthen the arms and shoulders, there's a tendency to bend the back, knees and hips as you become tired. The larger leg and back muscles help force the weight upward and take some of the burden off the arms and shoulders. Since the last few repetitions of any exercise are the most important, and this is where you are most likely to cheat by using other muscles, this lack of isolation robs the arms and shoulders of the desired train-ing. It's important to make sure that each exercise is done with proper form to ensure the greatest isolation possible.

A conflict can exist between isolating muscles to develop strength and simulating the specific motions of a sport or event. A remedy used successfully by many individuals is to adopt two training methods. Develop muscle strength through isolation training during the off-season, and use training that is similar or specific to the sport during pre-season. Strength decays slowly, so the off-season training should provide the strength base necessary for the coming season.

Strength is not gained at an even rate. The major success occurs early in an overload program. Typical increases of strength range from 5 to 12 percent a week.

But that high rate will not continue, because as you gain strength it takes progressively more effort and training to improve. After the initial surge, strength training gains follow a pattern of plateaus and small improvements. The improvements lessen more and more as you near your overall strength potential.

In strength training, the last few exercises in any set of repetitions are the most important. An overloaded muscle will fatigue after a few repetitions. As it tires, the exercises become harder and harder. This is the critical point in strength development, the point when you must discipline yourself to continue the exercise despite fatigue and pain. You also must discipline yourself to do each repetition with proper form. Do not squeeze out the last repetition by using other muscles or by rapidly accelerating the weights during the easiest portion of the exercise.

In order to make strength gains, the muscle must be pushed to the point where it will no longer perform. Only this will cause rapid strength gains in a muscle.

EXERCISE TYPES

Strength development can be accomplished using three types of exercises: isokinetic, isotonic and isometric. Each has its proponents and critics. The best advice is to use the method that is most aptly suited to your needs or most closely simulates the strength requirements of your sport.

In isometrics, the length of the muscle being exercised is not changed. Standing in a doorway and pushing out against the frame is an example of an isometric exercise. Another example is pushing your hands together in front of your chest for ten to fifteen seconds. Touted as "effortless" exercise because there is little need for equipment and because it can be done almost anywhere, isometrics gained great popularity a few years ago. That popularity has since faded.

Isometrics is not generally suggested for an active training program. While it may provide an opportunity for someone to exercise muscles while sitting at a desk, it has proven to be a less efficient method of developing strength. Also, the speed at which muscle contraction occurs cannot be improved with isometric training. The last problem is that there is no accurate method of measuring progress that is made. This is more important than it might sound, because measured improvements are the best incentives to work harder. For these reasons and because isometrics does not lend itself to aerobic strength programs, we will not discuss it further.

Isotonics is the exercise form most commonly associated with weight training. A constant weight or resistance is worked through a repetition. Working with dumbbells is a good example of an isotonic exercise.

Using isotonics, a muscle can be strengthened while either contracting or lengthening. Concentric exercising (with the muscle contracting) is much more popular than excentric (lengthening) exercising, though both are effective. Instead of pulling a weight up to overcome gravity, as in concentric exercising, in excentrics the weight is increased and the exerciser tries to resist the downward motion of the weight. This method, also known as negative lifting, offers the advantage of being able to use larger weight resistances, but it requires the assistance of at least one spotter at each station. Very few lifters use negative lifting techniques.

The major drawback of isotonic training is that, while the weight resistance remains constant through the exercise, the amount of work the muscle does to lift it varies considerably through the course of the lift. For example, picture a two-arm curl. Initially, moving the barbell is easy, since movement is parallel to the floor, not against gravity's pull. The muscle's work reaches a peak when the forearm and upper arm are at a ninety-degree angle. Although the weight has not changed, the exercise difficulty has.

This causes a tendency to accelerate the weight rapidly upward during the initial, easy phase. This is called the ballistic effect. The arm biceps get little or no work if the weight is thrown upward and not lifted. And, with ballistic effects, extraneous movement of the legs, hips or back will further reduce the training load on the arm biceps.

The ultimate result of this variance in workload is uneven and inefficient strength gains. The largest gains occur where the resistance is greatest. Also, the maximum weight that can be lifted is limited to the maximum that can be lifted through the weakest part, or the sticking point, of the repetition.

In an attempt to overcome this problem, elaborate equipment has been developed to mechanically adjust the resistance so that the load is held constant throughout the exercise range. Variable-resistance isotonic machines such as Nautilus and Dnya Cam are becoming increasingly popular.

Nautilus Equipment

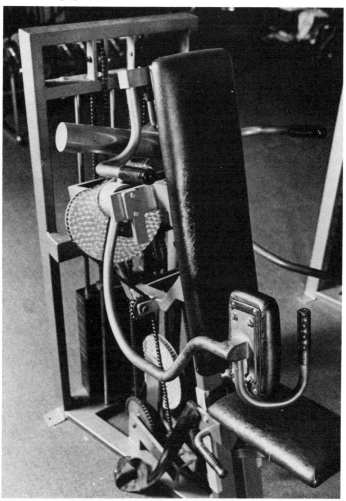

Nautilus equipment is bizarre-looking, but effective.

There are two factors to consider in use of variable-resistance isotonic machines. First, the machines are designed carefully to be very efficient at isolating particular muscles for exercise, including the use of variable seat heights, safety belts and complicated movements. They make it harder to cheat, that is, to use other muscles to complete an exercise. The effectiveness of muscle isolation results in more rapid strength gains. However, few sports are similar to the artificial movements used in these exercises. Although strength gains occur faster, you potentially lose the specifics of movements that mimic your sport.

The decision between variable isotonic machines and isotonic exercises is not an easy one. Isotonics provides more flexibility in program choice and offers a chance to exercise the muscles in movements that more closely parallel those in your sport. Although it may be possible to get some aerobic training effect while using variable isotonic equipment, it is rarely done. If you do use the heavy machinery of a variable-resistance program, augment it with a good stretching program and with exercises not included in the array of machines.

More often than not your choice will be dictated by the availability of equipment. Doing your workouts religiously is much more important than the type of equipment used.

The third exercise type, isokinetics, overcomes the problems of ballistics and variable resistance. In isokinetics, speed of movement is controlled by the machine. Pull as hard as you can or with a fraction of your strength, but the device still moves at the same speed. It is instantly adapted to your strength and eliminates variance of resistance throughout the range of motion. Also there is no ballistic problem, because acceleration, or the rate of increase in speed, is controlled.

Isokinetic machines are now heavily used in the evaluation and rehabilitation of injuries for professional athletics. They are also strongly suggested for athletes engaged in isokinetic sports, such as swimming.

Your choice of exercise type will vary according to your needs and desires. However, isotonics remains the most popular. Currently they are accessible to more people than many of the other types, and they are also the most adaptable to an aerobic strength training program. That's why most of the exercises in this book are isotonic.

TECHNIQUES

There are many strength training programs and all of them can be described in terms of sets and repetitions. A repetition is one continuous execution of an exercise, "rep" for short. A series of reps done without stopping is known as a set.

A typical description for a program would be three sets of ten reps.

The choice of exercise resistance or weights is based on achieving the reps and sets specified in your program. What's right for your exercise partner is not necessarily right for you.

A general guideline is to use enough weight so that you can barely achieve the desired number of repetitions. If you reach the upper limit of your repetition schedule, add more weight. If you cannot reach it, reduce the weight. The key is to do the number of repetitions that the program calls for. However, do not stop if you reach the number. Always do as many reps as you can. Drive the muscle to fatigue. If the number of reps you were able to do was different from the number specified in your program, change the weight accordingly, for your next set or workout.

If you are just starting a program, it is best to begin with very light weights. Concentrate on developing good exercise form, then increase the poundage later. Developing good form initially is a time investment that will pay great dividends as you continue to train. Poor form will haunt you for the duration of your program.

You can make an accurate determination of the optimum weights if you do several sets of the same exercise using different weights each time. Rest amply between the sets and record the number of repetitions you were able to perform.

On a graph, plot on the vertical axis the work done for each weight. The work completed is the weight multiplied by the number of repetitions you were able to do. Plot that weight on the horizontal axis.

Connect the points on your work curve to make a line. If you have chosen a wide range of weights, you will get a dome-shaped curve similar to the one shown earlier. The highest point represents the maximum work you did in that exercise. Points to the left of the maximum are in the underload zone. Points to the right are in the overload zone. When choosing weights, you want to be just to the right of the maximum, in the overload zone. That will ensure that you get efficient strength development. Training in the underload zone, even for extended periods, will not enhance your strength.

Another rule of thumb is that no strength gains will be achieved unless the weight is at least one third of your maximum strength for that exercise. This is the largest weight you can lift once, referred to as your 1 RM (repetition maximum). Care should be taken in trying to determine your maximum. Do not attempt it unless you have developed good form for the exercise.

We emphasize good exercise form, because if exercises are done poorly they loose their value and in some cases can cause physical harm. When you enter a good weight room you'll notice mirrors on several walls. They are there to help you attain good form. Watch yourself exercise to see where your form may be deteriorating. Even better, have friends who are working out with you critique your form.

To analyze your form, check for three elements—isolation, ballistic effect and movement through the entire range of motion. Is the proper muscle group doing the work or is it getting help from other muscles? Watch for extraneous movements. Are you throwing the weight, or accelerating it rapidly in the first part of each repetition? You should be moving the weights at a steady and controlled speed. Also, make sure that you perform the exercise through the full range of motion to maintain flexibility and to ensure consistent strength development throughout the range.

Here are a few mechanics of strength training. The most common grips are the overhand (pronated) and underhand (supinated)

Overhand Grip

The overhand grip shown with a barbell.

Underhand Grip

The underhand grip shown with a barbell.

grips. By changing grips with the same exercise, you often change the set of muscles being exercised. Use the grip specified in the exercise.

While performing exercises, keep your breathing natural. Exhale while contracting muscles or pushing the weights against gravity and inhale while relaxing your muscles. Do not hold your breath. In aerobic strength training, breathing form is not a problem—your body's demand for oxygen will ensure a strong breathing pattern.

It is important to schedule your workout so you can train consistently and follow a regular routine.

You should not work out on consecutive days, because then the exercised muscles will have no time to repair themselves and no strength gains will occur. The exception to using weights only on alternate days, as recommended, is if you follow a split routine. A split routine exercises one part of the body one day, another part the next day. A split routine might run like this:

Monday — Upper body exercises

Tuesday — Lower body exercises

Wednesday — No workout

Thursday — Upper body exercises

Friday — Lower body exercises

If you are not doing a split routine, the optimum number of strength workouts is three a week. You can use the off days for your hard aerobic workouts. Lay off strength training at least two days before important competition in a sport.

Always start your workout routine with a warmup and stretching exercises. Then take a few extra minutes to go to each exercise station to practice the movement of each exercise, using either no weight or very light weight. Then begin training.

If possible, structure the workout to exercise the larger muscles first, in this order—legs, hips, back, stomach, chest, shoulder, upper arms, ankles, forearms and neck.

Do the first couple of repetitions slowly to help avoid injury. Stretch your muscles when you are finished.

DESIGNING YOUR PROGRAM

What are your strength training goals? Great strength? Lots of endurance? One way to answer this question is to first ask: What are the demands of your sport? Do you want to improve your power on a tennis serve, strengthen your grip to make you a more effective judo competitor?

Except for the principles of specificity and overload, there are no hard and fast rules for strength training. There are, however, a variety of systems suggested to meet different goals. The number of reps and sets in your program will depend on your goals. When starting, try for eight to twelve repetitions. Use a weight light enough so you can do eight to twelve reps easily. After several workouts, adjust the number of reps and the weights to your desired program.

Here are some suggested reps and sets for various training goals:

Goals	Reps	Sets	Pace
Learning exercises	8 - 12	1 - 3	slow
Muscle strength	3 - 6	3 - 4	slow
Muscle endurance	15 - 20	3	medium
General muscle fitness	8 - 12	3	medium
Muscle power	8 - 15	1 - 2	fast

As in any strength program, the weights or exercise resistance should be chosen so that the number of repetitions specified in your program can be done when you are working hard.

Other programs recommend anywhere from one to six reps for strength and as many as fifty for endurance. Coaches have their own philosophies that will probably dictate your program. Use the guide initially; experiment from there to see what gives you the best results. We usually advocate not doing more than twenty or twenty-five repetitions and actually twelve to fifteen are probably sufficient for endurance. More reps would guarantee that you are not in the overload zone.

Current research indicates that endurance programs can build strength, as well as endurance, and that strength programs can also build endurance; however, only a few experiments have been conducted and the established procedures of low reps for strength and higher reps for endurance are still popular.

In a classic study, De Lorme and Watkins concluded that the following program offers the fastest gains in strength:

Set Number	Number of repetitions	Resistance
1	10	½ 10 RM
2	10	¾ 10 RM
3	10	10 RM

Ten RM, repetition maximum, is the heaviest weight that can be used to get just ten repetitions. One half 10 RM is one half of that weight. This program is thought to cause maximum hypertrophy—muscle growth. Other researchers have suggested reducing the number of reps and increasing the exercise resistance.

There are many exercise programs; however, few have been tested in controlled experiments. At this time we cannot say that one is necessarily better than the other. Here are a few programs. We recommend you start with progressive sets. Later you can change to any of the other systems.

Progressive Sets. There are two ways to progress in this program: increase the sets or increase the reps. If you start out doing a single set of exercises for two to three weeks, then add a second set and continue on that schedule for the same length of time until you add a third set. Don't worry about changing weight until you are doing all three sets. This program minimizes muscle soreness and allows you to develop good exercise form.

Double Progression. In double progression you start at three sets of exercises, with a low number of reps. Start with eight reps for arms and shoulders and twelve for legs, back and stomach. Increase the reps on a regular basis, for example one or two per week. Do not worry about increasing the weights until you are doing the desired number of reps through all three sets.

Start with light weights and every other workout add one rep to each set of arm and shoulder exercises and two to the other exercises. When you have reached a maximum of twelve reps for arms and shoulders and twenty for the other muscles, you can then increase the resistance.

Super Sets is an advanced program, advocated only for those who are interested in hypertrophy or muscle growth. The concept calls for doing a set of exercises for a particular muscle group and then, with no rest, doing a set for the antagonistic muscle group. For example, you do a triceps exercise closely followed by a biceps exercise. After working the antagonistic pair, rest for two or three minutes. Then repeat the procedure twice more. A program for Super Sets might consist of exercising the following pairs of antagonists.

biceps (curls)	triceps (press)
quadriceps (leg press)	hamstring (curls)
chest (flies)	upper back (reverse flies)

Pyramiding Super Sets. This is an example of combining two programs. Do Super Sets, but after each set increase the weights.

Testing your strength. By periodically testing your strength you can set short-term goals for yourself, evaluate progress and review your long-term goals. Comparing the present level of strength to that of previous tests can give you the incentive to continue your program. If your progress exceeds your expectations, you have earned a reward. Do something nice for yourself. If your progress is not up to pace, try to analyze why it is not. Were your goals too ambitious? Did you work consistently enough or hard enough?

Strength training, in preparation for a sport, can best be evaluated by your success in that sport. If your goal is to excel in a sport, strength training has application only as it helps you reach that goal. Thus the best test of strength for you comes not in a weight room, but in competing in your sport. Admittedly, there are many factors involved in improvement, so it may be hard to attribute it solely to strength training. But if you cannot convince yourself that your improved strength is helping your game, then why continue strength training?

In the weight room, one of the best ways to periodically retest yourself is to repeat the experiment that determined where your overload zone was. Use the same weight that you first used in your training program and see how many repetitions you can do. Plot this result on the original chart and keep it as a graphic display of your progress.

If you are especially interested in developing endurance strength, you could employ an endurance test. See how many repetitions, using a light weight, you can do in two minutes. Record both the weight and the number of reps. Later, repeat the test using the same weights.

The test for pure strength is the 1 RM. That is, the heaviest weight you can pump once. Be very careful taking this test, because the strain may lead to injury—especially to your back.

RULES FOR GAINING STRENGTH

We have discussed only a few of the many systems and programs for gaining strength. Go into any weight room and you will find a dozen others in use.

It is most probable that no one scheme for building strength is much better than another. That is true, as long as the basic principles are adhered to:

    1) isolate the specific muscle you want to strengthen

    2) give the muscle an exercise load greater than it is used to; overload the muscle.

    3) do repetitions until the muscle fatigues

    4) repeat sets

    5) repeat workouts.

The last rule, repeat workouts, is important to mention in the context of choosing a particular program. The best program for you is one you will repeat earnestly. If you find a program you like, stick with it. Be confident that you will get results through hard work and repetition.

PART TWO
THE PROGRAMS

4

Training Physiology

What happens to your body when you train? Typically we think first that a loss of body weight will occur. More precisely, we hope that the fat content will be reduced. Also, we expect the heart, lungs, circulatory system and muscles will somehow be improved. In this chapter we examine some of the effects of training on the body. Keep in mind this is a cursory look. More information can be obtained from the references listed at the end of this chapter.

WEIGHT CONTROL

The effect most often associated with physical training is weight loss. When you announce that you are embarking on a fitness program, the inevitable question arises: "Are you trying to lose weight?" The association is so strong that most people never get beyond this point.

Exercise can be an effective way to lose weight, but it isn't always. In simple terms it seems logical that if you increase your level of activity you will burn up more calories and thus lose more weight. Basically that is correct. However, during exercise you burn calories very slowly. You cannot normally go out and run off a few pounds. You may lose a few pounds while running, but most of that loss is water, which will return in the form of weight when you quench your thirst at a water fountain.

The fact that real weight loss is not due to sweating is still not widely understood. All too often people do strenuous exercise in

47

rubber or plastic suits to induce sweat. Their goals are to "sweat it off." Not only is the practice not effective, it is dangerous. Losing weight should mean losing calories of fat. That process is different from losing sweat, which is mostly water. The problem is not solved by avoiding drinking. Since your body needs water and cannot function without it, avoiding liquids will only lead to dehydration and might be harmful. Furthermore, the loss of sweat degrades exercise performance. By sweating heavily using artificial means you may not be able to run as far or as fast as you could under normal conditions. Thus, you could reduce your caloric expenditure during an exercise period by having to cut short the exercise period. Lastly, rubber suits shut off evaporation of sweat, which cools the body. Exercise generates heat (about 70 percent of the energy expended in exercise is heat, not movement) and with no way for the body to cool itself, body temperature will rise. Just a few degrees of elevated temperature can cause serious problems, leading to heat exhaustion or heat stroke.

The actual number of calories lost during exercise is surprisingly small. Running a mile burns up only about one-hundred calories. Since there are 3,500 calories in a pound, you would have to run thirty-five miles to lose one pound. Running is not a quick solution to an overweight problem. However, if you run thirty-five miles a week, you could lose fifty-two pounds over the span of one year. That is a substantial sum. The message here is that weight control is a long-term project—about a life time in length—and that exercise is important in weight control but does not provide a quick or easy solution.

There are additional weight-loss benefits to exercise, beyond the one-hundred calories expended per mile. At the end of an exercise period, your metabolic rate does not immediately return to its pre-exercise level. For as long as three or four hours after exercise your metabolic rate will be elevated. During that time your body consumes more calories than it would at rest. Further, exercise reduces appetite, contrary to what you might think. Thus, exercise may help you in decreasing your caloric intake.

The other method of losing weight is by dieting. It can be effective, especially when coupled with an exercise program. However, there are dangers in dieting. Fasting, which has been a recent fad, actually causes larger losses of lean body weight than fat body weight. Thus, although your weight may decrease, you are losing more muscle than fat. A second danger from dieting or fasting is that your health might suffer from the lack of needed nutrients. Reducing your caloric intake moderately while maintaining an exercise program is probably the best method of weight control.

Although most people look only at their bathroom scales to measure weight control, the composition of the body in terms of fat and muscle is a better measure. For example, if you start a strength training program your body weight may increase slightly after a couple of weeks training. That would not be cause for concern, because strength training reduces the fat content in muscles and increases their lean weight. Thus, although your weight may remain constant or even increase while in a strength training program, you will lose fat.

Measuring body fat is typically done in either of two ways. The easiest is to use calipers that measure the thickness of a fold of skin. This test is often administered at health clubs. It can be performed in a few minutes and gives fairly reliable estimates. Underwater weighing is far more accurate, but requires a special facility. Because fat tissue is lighter (less dense) than water, while lean tissue is heavier, tests have been devised that require the use of a swimming pool or laboratory tub. These tests provide a more meaningful measure of the loss or gain of body fat than does total body weight.

Exercise is not the total solution to weight control. However, tests have shown that obesity and physical activity are negatively correlated. That is, overweight people are generally less active. We do not know if slender people are slender because they are active or if they are active because they are slender. In either case, proper exercise continued over periods of months and years, is effective in controlling the accumulation of body fat.

INTERNAL ORGANS

A number of changes to the conditions of internal organs are brought about by exercise. We will present a few of the better-understood changes.

Vigorous exercise causes two different improvements in the capacity of the lungs to furnish oxygen to the circulatory system. First, the muscles that assist in breathing are strengthened by exercise. Air flow into the lungs is controlled by the difference in air pressures between the ambient air conditions and the conditions inside the lungs. The greater the pressure differential you can cause, the greater the resulting air flow will be. Muscles contract the lung cavity, putting pressure on the air in the lungs and forcing the air out. At the end of the expiration phase, the muscles relax and the lungs fill again, because the outside air pressure is greater than the reduced pressure inside. By strengthening the muscles that control breathing, the process of respiration becomes easier and more efficient.

Second, exercise also increases the usable space within the lungs. The space in the lungs is either residual volume or vital, usable capacity. Aerobic conditioning tends to yield a higher percentage of usable volume per lung volume. Although the lungs do not increase in size, their effective size is increased.

The heart undergoes three transformations as a result of exercise. The easiest measure of the condition or operation of the heart is the heart or pulse rate. The resting heart rate will decrease as conditioning improves through exercise. This means that your heart beats slower or less frequently and has an easier job. A trite rebuttal to strenuous exercise being good for you argues that it consumes valuable heartbeats, which supposedly are limited in number. It is fun to counter this argument by showing that exercise actually reduces the number of times your heart beats in a day. For example, you could lower your resting heart rate by ten beats a minute. It would take some time to achieve this reduction, but it is a realistic figure. That would save nearly fifteen thousand beats a day. To achieve that saving you might expend an additional eighty beats per minute for thirty minutes of exercise. Your cost would be a total of 2,400 beats, but your daily savings would be 12,600 beats. Even if you add some recovery time after exercise to allow your heart rate to return to normal, you might cut your net savings to ten thousand heartbeats a day. That is an impressive savings—one that shows the value of exercise for your heart. Finally, the volume of blood pumped in each stroke increases with improved conditioning. The ability of a heart to pump more blood with each contraction allows for the reduced pulse rate described above. There may also be an actual increase in the size and weight of the heart. Certainly the vascularization of the heart increases. That is, the heart itself becomes better supplied with blood vessels. The improved blood flow to any muscle, including the heart, makes it easier for that muscle to perform.

Other changes occur that make the heart's job easier. With the reduction in body fat, a benefit often associated with training, there is a reduction in the number of blood vessels, which were used to supply the fatty tissue. One estimate is that for each pound of fat lost, the circulatory system is shortened by one mile.

Blood vessels also become more pliable, which results in improved blood flow; and the heart has less work to perform. Exercise can reduce the total resistance to blood flow by as much as 50 percent. Reduced resistance causes reduced blood pressure.

Exercise also causes an increase in the volume of blood in the body. The total hemoglobin increases as the blood volume increases and thus the circulatory system's ability to carry oxygen is improved.

Another result of exercise, is the reduction of stress and improvement in the ability to handle stress. Participation in strenuous exercise can reduce the physiological affects of emotional stress. Some laboratory data supports this statement, as does the general consensus among runners and other regular exercisers.

Not to be left out, the digestive system benefits from physical exertion. The reduction in emotional stress also helps digestion by not producing excess acid in the stomach. Stronger muscles help bowel activity and vigorous exercise is one of the best natural laxatives.

MUSCLES

What happens to muscles when they undergo strength training? The common answer is that they get larger or hypertrophy. Although this certainly occurs, hypertrophy is linked both to the intensity and continuity of workouts and is limited by genetic factors. Few women (one in twenty) experience noticeable enlargement of muscles from strength training. Many men do not experience major changes, either. For most people it would be difficult to appreciably increase their musculature. Nonetheless, hypertrophy does occur, although the changes may be slight.

There are several mechanisms that cause hypertrophy. The most important is the increase in the diameter of individual muscle fibers. This occurs because there is an increase in the number of units making up each muscle fiber. It has long been thought that the number of fibers does not change—only the size of each fiber increases. Some recent research indicates that this view may be wrong and that the fibers may split longitudinally, forming new fibers.

The fibers in a muscle may have different diameters. Strength training will cause the smaller fibers to enlarge. Thus, although the size of the largest fibers may not change, strength training develops more large fibers from smaller ones.

The amount of protein in the muscle increases. Also, the strength of connective tissues, ligaments and tendons increases. The density of capillaries increases. This last effect is very important in building endurance and reducing muscle fatigue. The increased ability to supply oxygen to, and remove waste products from muscles increases muscular endurance.

Hypertrophy is positively correlated with strength. The empirical relationship between hypertrophy and strength is the same for men and women. Thus, hypertrophy accompanies strength gains but you should not expect big bulging muscles. Muscles that are allowed to grow weaker through disuse, get smaller as they get weaker. Your loss of strength occurs at the rate of about 1 percent per day.

In hypertrophy the muscle fibers are what change size. When performing any task, the strength provided by a muscle reflects the number of fibers that are used. Each fiber is either contracting or not contracting. For easy tasks, or light loads, few of the fibers are called on to perform the task. For heavier jobs, more fibers are used. Strength training increases the work output of each of the fibers and improves the ability to recruit fibers.

One result of training removed from muscle strength is that the nervous system learns to mobilize more motor units. Thus, without an actual increase in strength, the amount of work performed can be increased with better nervous control of the muscles. This occurs by exhausting the muscle fibers, giving them time to recover and exhausting them again (repeating repetitions, sets and workouts). When someone first starts a strength training program, much of the early improvement comes from increased ability to mobilize motor units.

Strength gains can occur as rapidly as 12 percent per week. If this high rate continued, you would double your strength every six weeks. This, unfortunately, will not occur. The stronger you get, the slower your strength gains will occur. Ultimately, your genetic makeup and dedication to training will limit your gains.

One other effect on muscles occurs: soreness. When beginning a strength program, or when you add exercises for muscles that have not been regularly exercised, you will experience muscle soreness.

Soreness is related to the incomplete removal of exercise waste products from the muscle. The removal process will quickly improve with continued exercise. The soreness is not a signal that you should stop exercising. In fact, if you do abstain until the soreness vanishes, your muscles may not develop the ability to rid themselves of wastes. Thus, each time you start you will be sore again. So continue your program and the soreness will soon go away.

FACTORS AFFECTING STRENGTH

Although your strength training program will develop strength, you will not be able to perform the same level of work at all times. Several factors control the strength a muscle can provide. There is a diurnal variation in strength. Strength is at a minimum early in the morning but rises to its maximum value within a few hours. It declines again in the late evening. Some experiments have shown seasonal changes in strength. Researchers found subjects to be weakest in January and February and strongest in September and October. Temperature also affects strength. Slight warming may increase strength and cooling decreases it. Of course, psychological factors can also be important.

REFERENCES

de Vries, H.A. *Physiology of Exercise for Physical Education and Athletics.* Wm. C. Brown Company, Dubuque, Iowa, 1966.

Matthews, D.K. and E.L. Fox. *The Physiological Basis of Physical Education and Athletics.* W.B. Saunders Company, Philadelphia, 1976.

5

Exercises

Although there are many exercises that can be performed without weights or weight machines, we recommend them for exercises in aerobic strength training programs. Weights give you the ability to isolate muscle groups for an intensive workout and the ability to adapt exercise resistance to almost any level of strength. Of course, when you don't have access to weights you can substitute comparable exercises that do not require them.

We have talked about isolation of muscles as one of the fundamental principles in effective strength training. It is very difficult to devise exercises that can *totally* isolate single muscles, however. Even in the simplest of motions, many muscles are involved.

So, in choosing exercises think about training and isolating individual motions rather than single muscles. You can devise exercises to work the muscles in three planes of motion that are important to your sport. By thinking about how each part of your body moves or rotates, you can more easily learn what motions should be mimicked in strength training.

For example, motions of the lower arm relative to the upper arm are restricted by the elbow joint. You can bend (flex) the arm or straighten (extend) it. Extension is accomplished by two muscles, while flexing requires four. There is no need to memorize the names of these six muscles to strengthen them. Because the elbow joint restricts the movement to extension and flexion, you need to include only two exercises.

The exercises presented in this chapter have been divided into ten exercise groups, based on motions of the body. These ten groups are subdivided into subgroups of opposing muscles. In general, both members of an opposing muscle group should be exercised. For example, if you are exercising the arm flexors, you should also exercise the extensors. This is to prevent muscle imbalance and injury.

We describe motion in terms of flexion and extension, and abduction and adduction. Flexion is movement of one limb or body part toward another; extension is the separation of two parts. In abduction, the motion is away from the centerline of your body. Raising your foot to the side (while keeping the leg straight) is abduction of the leg. Bringing the leg back toward centerline is adduction.

Some muscles allow a third type of motion—rotation. You can rotate your body while keeping your feet fixed.

The ankle is capable of motion around three axes. Bringing the toes up is called ankle flexion. Pushing them down is called ankle extension. Inversion is the process of rotating the foot up to the inside and eversion is the action of pulling it up to the outside. The ankle joint also allows horizontal rotation: you can rotate your feet while they are flat on the floor.

These terms will be used to identify exercises instead of using names of the muscles. Training is less complicated if you remember motions and not muscles.

Of course it is useful to learn the names of muscles, but it is not necessary. Common muscle names are given here for most of the exercises.

Exercises within each subgroup are given in order, depending on the equipment needed. We have included several variations of most exercises to accommodate various availabilities of equipment.

EQUIPMENT

A set of dumbbells and barbells is essential for almost any strength program. They can be used alone, but more often complement weight machines. Barbells and dumbbells are inexpensive and versatile, which makes them ideal if you work out at home.

Dumbbells are hand-held, one in each hand. They can either be fixed-weight (usually in five-pound increments) or variable-weight. Barbells consist of a steel bar, spacing sleeve, locking collars and weights. Collars ensure that the weights will not slip off.

Weight machines are complex and expensive. There are more than a dozen major manufacturers of weight machines, the most common type being an isotonic machine using pulleys or levers, such as a Universal machine. Cam machines, of which Nautilus is one, are growing in popularity. They are variable-resistance, isotonic machines. To vary the resistance they use an unsymmetric cam. In isokinetic machines, hydraulic systems or governors are used to control the speed of movement.

One piece of equipment that frequently is not found in the gym but that may be very helpful is an iron boot or ankle weight. It allows you to do many leg exercises that have application in a variety of sports.

All of this equipment can be used in aerobic strength training; however, equipment that requires making adjustments for seat position as well as for exercise resistance, or that requires the use of seat belts or other restraining devices, is not applicable. It takes too long to make the adjustments, during which time your heart rate drops below the training minimum. A possible way around this is to have a partner make the adjustments and set the weights.

The kind of equipment is not critical in aerobic strength training, except when one piece of equipment closely mimics motions of your sport. Much more important than the type of equipment is your selection and performance of exercises.

EXERCISES

The following exercises are divided into ten muscle groups based on joint motion. They are listed in the suggested training sequence of working on strongest muscles first. They are further divided by the equipment on which they may be performed. A sequence of stretches for the groups is given at the end of this chapter. Refer to the drawings for the names of muscles.

LOWER LEG

Motion of the lower leg is controlled by the muscles in the upper leg, the quadriceps and the hamstring groups. Strength here is essential for providing knee stability and protecting it from injury. The quadriceps (front of the leg) are the strongest of the two groups and are emphasized in most sports.

Leg Extension

Leg extensor muscles are located along the front of the thigh. Conceptually, there are two ways to strengthen these muscles: you may apply resistance to the front of the lower leg at the ankle and push the leg out straight. Or, extend your legs, as in standing up from a kneeling position.

Isotonic or isokinetic machines — Seat yourself on the edge of the bench of a thigh-and-leg machine and hook your feet under the weights. Grip the edges of the bench and raise your legs parallel to the floor. Let them down slowly. On isotonic machines, move at a steady pace throughout. Do not jerk the weights upward in the initial movement of the exercise. To help counteract this, pause at full extension for a second before lowering the weights, and work against the weights as they come back down.

Ankle weights, iron boot — You can use this exercise at home with an iron boot or ankle weights. A heavy boot with bricks tied to it can also be used for an iron boot.

With barbells — Squats should be done with care, since deep, full squats can place too great a strain on knee joints.

Keep your head up, back arched and feet shoulder-width apart.

Squats

Be careful with Squats. The knees take much of the strain.

Keep your head up, back arched.

With the bar resting on your shoulders, bend your knees until your thighs are parallel to the floor. Then stand up.

One method of making sure you will not go too deep with the squat, thus jeopardizing your knees, is to put a bench or chair behind you. This ensures you will stop when you hit the half-squat position. For better stability during squats, stand with your heels on a two-by-four and your toes on the floor.

Isotonic leg press machines — Position the seat so that your legs are bent at a ninety-degree angle, to begin. Place your feet squarely on the pedals and your back flat on the chair. Hold yourself in this position so that you press the weights up.

Using the step — Find a step so that when you place one foot on it, your thigh is parallel to the floor. If you're over five feet tall. use a twelve-inch step. Those over six feet should use an eighteen- to twenty-inch step. Step up, placing the other foot on the step, too. Complete the set for one leg before starting the other leg. To increase the weight slightly, hold a dumbbell in one hand. Use your other hand to steady yourself.

Leg Flexion

Flexing the lower leg is done by the muscles of the hamstring group. These muscles are located along the back of the upper leg. They are difficult to exercise without weights.

Isotonic machines — Hamstring curls are usually performed on the same machine used for leg extensions. Lie prone and hold onto the bench; hook your legs under the pads and try to touch your buttocks with your heels. Pull smoothly and strive for full contraction. Rest your chin, not your cheek, on the bench to ensure sideways balance in the contraction.

Iron boot or ankle weights — Attach the weight to your foot and flex your legs. This can be done either while standing or lying on your stomach. The maximum effort occurs when the lower leg is horizontal. The two different exercise positions allow you to strengthen different ranges of motion.

No equipment — Lie on your back and bend your knees. Draw

Leg Flexion

Drawing your feet along the ground works the hamstrings.

your feet along the ground toward your buttocks. You can apply more resistance by putting weight on your legs by raising your buttocks off the ground.

UPPER LEG

Extension of the upper leg is the movement of the legs to the rear. Flexion is pulling the legs forward, as in kicking a ball.

Upper Leg Extension

The large muscles in the buttocks (gluteus maximus) are primarily responsible for pulling the legs back. The hamstrings play a secondary role along the back of the upper leg.

Isotonic machines — Grasp the foot braces on the back extension station or rest your chest on a tall table and hold onto the

Nautilus Hip and Back Machine

The Nautilus Hip-and-Back machine works the hip flexors.

Your legs are held straight up to begin the movement.

cont'd next page

Nautilus Hip and Back Machine (cont'd)

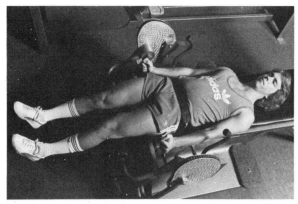

Push against the pads. Bring your feet as far down as possible.

sides. Raise both your legs together, with knees held straight, as high as possible. Then lower them slowly until the toes touch the

You can also work one leg at a time.

This is called the swimmer's kick.

cont'd next page

Nautilus Hip and Back Machine (cont'd)

Alternate legs.

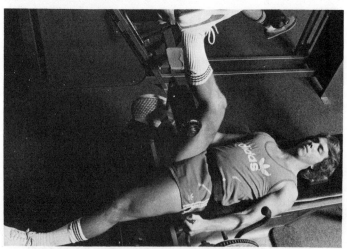

Work through the full range of motion on the machine.

floor. Do not accelerate in the first moments of this exercise. This is the swimmer's kick. Nautilus has an excellent machine (the hip-and-back machine) designed to exercise the hip extensor.

No equipment — Hold onto a doorknob or railing that is waist-high. Bend ·at the waist until your back is horizontal, steadying yourself by holding onto the railing. Raise one leg behind you as high as you can, keeping the knee straight. Do the desired repetitions before switching legs. An alternative is to stand on your toes facing a wall. Raise one leg behind you as high as possible, keeping the knee straight. Add ankle weights to increase the resistance on any of these exercises.

Upper Leg Extension Without Equipment

An upper leg extension without weights.

Upper Leg Flexion

This is one muscle group that usually does not need much strengthening. The hip flexors are usually strong and get exercise in many types of workouts and sports. Overdevelopment of these muscles may lead to back pain.

No equipment — Sit-up boards can be used but are not needed for these exercises. A good way to strengthen this group is to do straight-leg raises while lying on your back on the floor. Raise both legs, keeping the knees straight, until the hips rise off the floor. Then lower your legs slowly. Leg raises can also be done while standing (one leg at a time) or while hanging from a chin-up bar (both legs bent or straight at the knee).

Double Leg Raise

Keep the legs straight during a double leg raise.

Straight-leg sit-ups also provide more exercise for the hip flexors than for the abdominal muscles for which they are usually intended. To strengthen the hip flexors, do sit-ups with the feet anchored so they cannot move. For abdominal development, do the sit-ups with knees bent and without anchoring your feet.

Upper Leg Abduction and Adduction

Abduction is movement away from the center of the body. Adduction is movement toward it. Exercises for these muscle groups are seldom included in strength programs, but have particular value for some sports, such as skiing.

No equipment − The abductor group can be exercised while lying on your side, on the floor or on an inclined bench. Lift one leg upward directly above the other leg. This is the lateral leg raise. A variation requires a partner. Lie on your back with your legs straight and together. Push your feet away from each other while your partner resists with his hands. His resistance should be light enough so that you can gradually overcome the pressure.

For the adductor group, sit on the floor with your legs bent and feet flat on the floor. Grab your knees with your hands. Force your knees apart with your hands while resisting with your

Lateral Leg Raise

A lateral leg raise works the abductor muscles in the leg.

Leg Abduction

For leg abduction with a partner: overcome his hand resistance as you spread your legs.

adductors. A partner can also be used, in an exercise similar to that for the abductor group. Lie on the floor with legs straight. Bring your heels together while your partner resists with his hands.

Leg Adduction

Force your knees apart for working adductor muscles.

Leg Adduction with a Partner

With partner, for adductors, overcome resistance while bringing legs together.

THE TRUNK

Exercises of the trunk can prevent lower backaches and pains. While back muscles generally get very little exercise, they are sometimes called upon to perform extensively by the weekend athlete. Some back pain can result from having weak abdominal muscles. As the abdominal muscles weaken, the muscles of the lower back must constantly work to keep the spine erect. Fatigue of the back muscles causes back pain.

Trunk Extension

These muscles that extend the trunk lie along the back and pull against the hips.

Isotonic machines — Many multi-station machines have a back extension station. Rest your lower stomach on the pad and hook your heels under the padded block provided. With hands behind your head, lower your trunk as far as possible. Raise it up slowly as far as possible and hold this position for a full second. Oppose gravity on the downward motion. Also, do not accelerate during the early stages of the extension. If you do, you could overstretch your back. You can increase the resistance by holding a barbell weight behind your head. Hold it tightly, so that you don't bang your head.

Barbell or no equipment — The simplest exercise for the back muscles is toe touches. Stand with feet close together and knees straight. Bend at the waist as far as possible. To increase resistance, hold a weight or barbell. Start with the bar alone and add weight very sparingly. It is easy to exceed your lifting ability with this exercise.

The hip raise is another exercise that can be done without equipment. From a sitting position on the floor, support your weight on your feet and hands, keeping your knees tightly bent. Raise your hips so that your thighs and back are in a straight line.

Hip Raise

For the hip raise, keep knees bent, back straight.

Trunk Flexion

It is much more difficult than you might imagine to exercise the abdominal muscles. This is because in many exercises for the abdominals, other muscles end up doing most of the work.

The abdominal muscles are seen, when flexed on well-conditioned individuals, as two bands of rippled muscle, extending from the ribs to the waistline. They are assisted by the oblique abdominal muscles, connecting the lower four to eight ribs to the hips.

No equipment – The sit-up is the most common form of exercise for the abdominals, but care must be taken to ensure that you're actually working the muscles you intend to. Doing sit-ups with straight legs and your feet held by a strap or bar provides exercise primarily for the hip flexors instead of the abdominals. The hip flexors are usually already much stronger than their opposing muscle group and do not need an extra workout.

One way of isolating the abdominal muscles is to keep the knees bent. This position contracts the hip flexors and makes it harder for them to assist the abdominals. Keeping the knees bent also helps keep the back flat on the sit-up board or floor.

Sit-Ups

A standard sit-up begins from the prone position.

cont'd next page

Sit-Ups (cont'd)

Knees are bent, hands behind head.

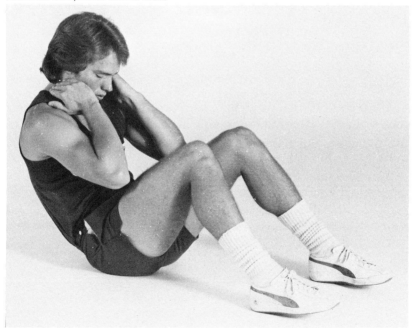

Sit-ups work the stomach muscles.

cont'd next page

Sit-Ups (cont'd)

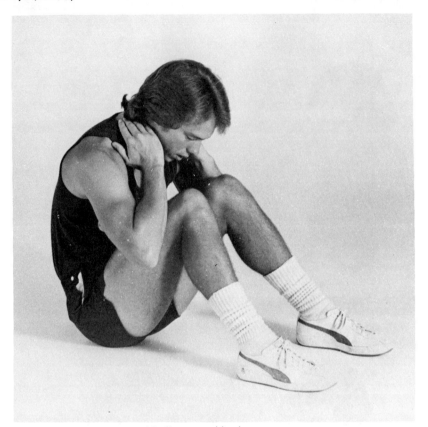

End the upward movement with elbows touching knees.

You can further isolate the abdominal muscles by not using a foot restraint. When you lock your feet under a strap or piece of furniture, the hip flexors can pull against the legs. Without such restraint the hip flexors are not as effective.

Another common fault in sit-up technique is using the head or arms to help accelerate the body upward. Putting your hands behind your head will help reduce this problem, though you might tend to start swinging your elbows up as the stomach muscles tire.

This can be a significant problem, because the angle at which the abdominals are best exercised is the first few degrees of movement. A rapid upward jerk at the start robs the abdominals of much of their training work.

If you tend to throw your body upward, try doing sit-backs instead of sit-ups. From a sitting position with your hands either behind your head or across your chest, sit back while slowly counting to ten. Sit up quickly and repeat.

Since full sit-ups are difficult to do with knees bent and feet flat on the floor, you might try an easier exercise—the partial sit-up or abdominal curl. With your hands behind your head, slowly curl up far enough to lift your shoulder blades off the floor. Hold the position for a second, then uncurl.

There are many variations of a sit-up. To make it more difficult, you can elevate your feet, on a chair for example. Or you can start from a position of lying flat on your back and pulling your knees up as you do a sit-up. Remember to not anchor your feet in these or other variations and to do the exercise smoothly, without jerking motions.

Leg raises are often used to strengthen abdominals, but like sit-ups, they are usually better exercise for the hip flexors than the stomach muscles. Leg raises should be done in a short range of motion, from the point where the knees meet the nose to the point where the hips meet the floor. An easy way to do this exercise is to keep your knees bent at ninety degrees. Your downward motion will stop when your feet hit the floor. To increase difficulty, keep your legs straight, but stop downward progress when your hips hit the floor.

With equipment. There are only a few trunk flexion exercises that require equipment. Nautilus has recently introduced an abdominal machine that may be effective at isolating the trunk flexors. Traditional equipment used in exercising these muscles includes barbell weights, the back extension station or the Roman chair. Weights can be used to increase the difficulty of ordinary sit-ups. Hold the weights behind your head. The other equipment can be used to allow deep sit-ups. These involve hyperextending the back and are not recommended for the novice. Make sure your back is flexible before trying them. In general we favor regular sit-ups that are done on the floor, to the alternatives.

LOWER ARM

The size of a person's biceps or triceps of the arm is often taken as a measure of overall strength. For that reason, many people overindulge in exercises for these muscles, while letting others go unused. The motion of the lower arm is restricted by the elbow and controlled primarily by the biceps and triceps.

Lower Arm Extension

No equipment — The most popular exercise is the push-up.

This exercise provides an opportunity to vary the muscles used, depending on hand spacing. It also offers the ability to change resistance, something unusual for exercises that do not use weights.

If you place your hands far apart, the pectorals (chest muscles that connect to the upper arm) do much of the work. Narrow hand spacing favors development in the triceps. Part of the deltoid muscle (top of the shoulder—upper arm) also helps.

Push-Ups

Narrow hand placement concentrates on the triceps.

Wide hand placement works the pectorals.

The standard push-up starts with the body being supported on the toes and the palms of the hands, placed about shoulder-width apart. The back is straight, feet together and the fingers point straight ahead. Lower your body by bending at the elbows until your chest touches the floor. Then push back up. Keep your head up, not facing down, and the elbows close to your sides.

Push-Ups (cont'd)

Standard push-up position to start.

Keep the back straight and lower your chin to the floor.

You can reduce the resistance required for this exercise by doing partial push-ups, from the knees. Use the knees for support instead of the toes. You can also reduce resistance by elevating the arms on a sofa or chair. Still too hard? Try doing push-ups against a wall. If you wish to increase resistance, elevate the feet. The higher you go the more you work the deltoids.

You can work on the pectorals by widening the hand stance and turning the hands outward.

Another arm extensor exercise that does not require weights is dips. A dipping station on a machine, parallel bars or two stable chairs can be used.

Starting from a position where you're supporting your weight on your arms, bend at the elbows until the upper arm is horizontal. Then push back up. Don't swing your body forward or backward.

Using chairs, let your feet rest on the floor or on a third chair

Partial Push-Ups

To do a partial push-up, rest your knees on the floor.

Keep your butt down as you lower to the floor.

Push-Ups Using a Chair

Push-ups with your feet propped up on a chair increase resistance.

cont'd next page

Push-Ups Using a Chair (cont'd)

This push-up requires considerable strength.

in front of you. Lower yourself as far as is comfortable, then push back up.

Barbell or dumbbells — The bench press is the most common form of exercise using weights, and as with push-ups, the width of the grip on the bar determines which muscles do the work. A wide grip works the pectorals. A narrow grip isolates the arm extensors.

Bench Press with a Barbell

Begin the barbell bench press with the bar on your chest.

Bench Press with a Barbell (cont'd)

Push the barbell straight up; do not arch your back.

A bench press is done while lying on an exercise bench. Place your feet flat on the floor. If you are shorter than five feet four inches, it may be more comfortable to place your feet flat on the bench. The important thing is that you do not arch your back or push with your feet.

The weight bench is equipped with a rack to hold the barbell and weight, however it will probably still be necessary to have a spotter, who helps you at the start and end of each set by grabbing the barbell and returning it to the rack. If you do not have a spotter and cannot get the bar off your chest, roll it up to your waist. Then sit up and roll it off your legs, onto the bench.

It is important to exercise through the full range of motion in the bench press. Do not try to squeeze out a few extra "reps" by failing to lower the bar fully. Remember, the benefits of the exercise apply only in the range of motion in which it is done.

The military press is done from a standing or sitting position. If you do it from a standing position, make sure that you do not bend your back or legs.

In the military press, grab the bar with an overhand grip and raise it up from the floor into the starting position. The hands should be about shoulder-width apart. Pull the barbell up to your chin with your elbows out to the side. Then drop your elbows down under the bar and get into a position where you are ready to press. If you can't get into this position, decrease the weight.

There are two variations of the military press. One is to lower the bar behind your head instead of in front of it.

Touch the bar to the back of your neck and then press upward. This variation works the rear part of the deltoid muscle, which is not worked in the other variation.

Standing Military Press

Place your hands wide on the barbell to begin the military press.

cont'd next page

Standing Military Press (cont'd)

Using an overhand grip, lift the bar to your shoulders.

Then, from the shoulders, begin the push upward, which starts a repetition.

Push the weight directly over your head.

You may lower the weight behind your head, to complete the movement, or back to your shoulders.

Another variation uses an inclined bench. This procedure makes it more difficult to cheat by using other muscles. The press is performed in the same way as the regular military press.

All of these exercises can be done using dumbbells, as well. Use an overhand grip and alternate pushing one up and bringing the other one down.

The triceps press is done with a barbell by resting the bar on your shoulders. Use an overhand grip closer than your shoulder width. Keep elbows together and press the bar up over your head and return.

Isotonic machines — The differences between using barbells, dumbbells or weight machines for these exercises are small. You will be able to press a heavier weight with a machine, because the weights are confined to travel in only one plane of motion and you do not have to balance the weight.

If you are doing a bench press on a machine, you will start with the arms in a flexed (lowered) position. Exhale as you push up. Also remember that although you may push more weight on a machine, the lifting action may not be as natural as that with a barbell. Using a barbell, if one arm pushes harder than the other, the bar will tilt and you will have to push with the other hand to bring the bar back to horizontal. With a machine, one arm can push harder than the other without you knowing it. Some machines have split bars so that each arm lifts independently of the other, which helps to eliminate that problem.

Bench Press at a Universal Gym

Narrow grip for bench press on Universal machine.

Wide grip for bench press on Universal machine.

cont'd next page

Bench Press at a Universal Gym (cont'd)

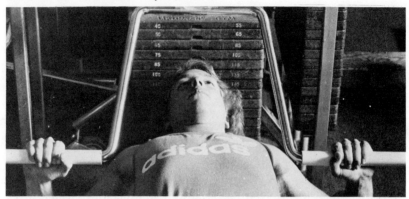

Start the bench press with arms in a lowered position.

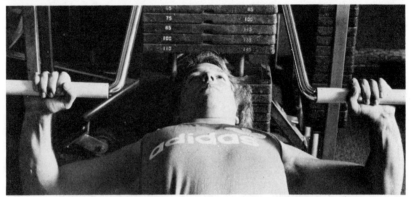

Drive the bars upward.

Do not arch your back or use your feet.

If you wish to do the behind-the-neck variation of the military press on a weight machine station, you must turn around to face the direction opposite to that for the regular military press.

Military Press at a Universal Gym

Begin the military press on a Universal machine with arms lowered.

Drive the weight upward.

Push to full extension. You may do this exercise standing or seated.

Most isotonic machines also offer a lat machine station, at which you can do a triceps press. Grab the bar with the hands close together in an overhand grip. Keep the elbows tucked in at your sides, and without moving the upper arm, press the bar down until your arms are extended.

Triceps Press at a High Lat Station

Begin the triceps press on the Universal machine with arms at chest level.

Keep your arms close together as you pull against the resistance.

Keep your elbows tucked and press down until your arms are fully extended.

The triceps exercise on cam-type isotonic machines is particularly well-isolated. You position your elbows on a padded block and extend your arms without any other body motion.

Nautilus Triceps Press

Place your forearms on the pads of the Nautilus triceps press.

With elbows anchored, push against the resistance.

Remain seated as you push the pads.

Your arms should be fully extended at the farthest point in the movement.

Lower Arm Flexion

The biceps muscle on the front of the arm is most commonly associated with arm flexion. However, two other muscles, the brachioradialis and brachialis (attached to the upper and lower arm bones) also contribute to the motion.

No equipment — Chin-ups are excellent. Grab a high bar with an underhand grip and the hands about shoulder-width apart. From a free-hanging position, pull yourself up until your chin is even with the bar, then lower yourself to a hanging position. Do not swing or kick your feet to help force yourself up. As you widen the grip, the latissimus dorsi muscles (those in the back which pull the upper arms down) become involved.

Chin-Ups

Use the underhand grip for standard chin-ups.

Pull yourself up and touch your chin to the bar.

Those who find full chin-ups too difficult may do partial chin-ups using a low bar (chest-high or lower). Grab the bar from beneath with an overhand grip. Swing under the bar with your feet far enough in front of you that you get a comfortable amount of weight on your arms. Leave your feet on the ground and legs straight. Pull yourself up until your chin touches the bar. You can vary the exercise difficulty if you have access to bars of several different heights.

Barbells and dumbbells — Rows and curls are the most common exercises for arm flexion. They are similar, only the grip is reversed.

Arm curls all use an underhand grip. While standing, hold the barbell with your hands and feet shoulder-width apart. Curl your wrists and arms upward, bringing the barbell to your chest as you exhale. Lower the weights slowly. Do not rock back and forth. Curls can also be done from a seated position, which eliminates extraneous movement.

Curls can be done with dumbbells, again using an underhand grip. Arm motion is alternated while doing dumbbell curls. Improve isolation by doing dumbbell arm curls over an inclined bench.

By reversing the grip to an overhand grip and moving the hands closer together on the barbell you can do upright rows. The exercise involves several other muscles that raise the arms, and is considered in more detail in discussion of the following muscle groups,

Arm Curls

Arm curls use an underhand grip.

Begin at your waist, lifting the bar to your shoulders before lowering back to your waist.

Dumbbell Curls

Curls with dumbbells use the same underhand grip as with a barbell.

You may alternate arm motion doing dumbbell curls.

where its application is greatest.

UPPER ARMS

Motions Toward and Away from the Chest

While the muscle groups that pull the arms together across the chest are frequently included in exercise programs at the bench press station, opposing muscle groups that pull the arms apart and away from the body are frequently ignored. This oversight can lead to a muscle imbalance that results in drooping shoulders and ill-fitting clothing.

Abductors of the Arms — Abduction of the arms requires a complex combination of movement by several muscles, including the trapezius (the triangular-shaped muscle that covers most of the back), the rhomboids (beneath the trapezius, which pull the shoulder blades toward the spine) and the latissimus dorsi, teres major and teres minor groups (which attach to the upper arm and pull it back toward the spine).

No weights — There are a couple of exercises that can be done without weights. One requires a chest expander, a set of springs attached to two handles, available at sporting goods stores. Pull the springs apart in front of your chest, keeping the elbows locked. In the second exercise, a partner takes the place of the chest expander, a set of springs attached to two handles, available at sporting goods stores. Pull the springs apart in front of your chest, keeping the elbows locked. In the second exercise, a partner takes the place of the chest expander. He places his hands outside yours and opposes as you spread your arms.

Barbells, dumbbells — One of the best exercises is the bent row. Remember, rows use an overhand grip, the opposite of curls.

Starting from a standing position, keep your back bent and horizontal and bend your knees. With the hands separated as far as possible, raise the bar to your chest and lower it at a controlled rate. Start with a light weight and increase it gradually.

The same exercise can be done with dumbbells. Start at the same position while holding a dumbbell in each hand. Alternate raising and lowering them.

The last exercise is the bent lateral raise, commonly known as reverse flies. In this exercise you bend at the waist, keeping the knees and back bent. Using a pair of light dumbbells, hold them so that your palms face each other. With the elbows straight, raise the dumbbells out to the side as far as possible.

It is important to raise the weights at a slow and steady pace. The resistance becomes progressively greater as your arms move farther out to the sides, producing a tendency to accelerate the weight initially in the exercise.

An exercise that overcomes the tendency to accelerate is the double arm pull on Nautilus equipment. From a seated position,

Upright Rows

Note hand position for upright rows.

Bent Rows

Bent rows call for hands being spread as far as possible on the bar.

Pull the weight toward your chest.

Keep your back bent, legs straight.

Bent Rows with Dumbbells

Dumbbells can be used for bent rows.

Work one arm.

Reverse Flies

Then work the other arm.

Reverse flies require dumbbells.

Begin with dumbbells together and then bring them out and up to your side, keeping the arms straight.

press outward with each arm, rotating the apparatus to the rear. The machine isolates the exercise well. Those who use Nautilus equipment should do this exercise to balance the strengthening of the chest or pectoral muscles, which oppose the abductors.

Adductors of the Arms

The pectoral muscles across the front of the chest are those most involved with moving the arms in front of the body. The pectoralis major attaches to the collarbone and sternum and to the upper arm bone near the shoulder. With the help of the pectoralis minor (which lies beneath the pectoralis major) and one part of the deltoid muscle, it pulls the arms in front of the chest.

Many of the exercises for this group were included in the analysis of exercises for strengthening extensors of the lower arm. To exercise the adductors, use a wider grip.

Flies

Use a bench to do flies.

The bend in the elbows reduces stress in that joint.

Lower the dumbbells to the floor and bring them over your head.

No equipment — Wide-grip push-ups are the most common exercise. Spread your hands wider than shoulder width. Rotate the position of hands outwards to forty-five degrees.

Barbell or dumbbells — The bench press station can be used to isolate the arm adductors by using a wide grip. Body position remains the same—on your back on the bench with your head supported. The recommended breathing pattern is to inhale either when your arms are fully extended or while you are flexing them. Exhale while exerting maximum effort. The wider spacing will probably force you to reduce the weight you can use.

A second exercise with dumbbells is the supine lateral raises commonly known as flies. Lie on your back on a bench, holding dumbbells on the floor with your palms facing up. Bend the elbows slightly and raise the weights directly over your chest. Then lower them to the floor and repeat. The bend in the elbows relieves stress on that joint.

UPPER ARM

Vertical Motions

There are four motions covered in this group of exercises: raising arms (vertical abduction), pulling them down (vertical adduction) and elevating and lowering the shoulder.

Vertical Abduction

The primary muscle involved in moving the arm upward is the deltoid, attached to the collarbone and upper arm bone. The deltoid is further divided into three parts. The middle pulls the arm up. The front and back parts pull the arm up and forward or backward.

Barbells or dumbbells — A lateral raise performed with dumbbells effectively isolates the middle portion of the muscle. From a standing position with the weights at your side, raise them until they are overhead, then lower them at a slow and steady rate.

To emphasize the front part of the deltoid, hold the dumbbells in front of you instead of directly to the side. Use an overhand grip and keep the knuckles facing upward.

Rowing exercises can also benefit the deltoids, though other muscle groups are involved. For the upright row, start by standing, then grab the bar with an overhand grip with your hands close together. Keeping your elbows out to the side, raise the bar

Lateral Arm Raise

The lateral raise works the middle portion of the upper arm.

Raise the dumbbells over your head.

Lower the weights at a slow, steady rate.

smoothly to your chin and return to the starting position. Don't let the bar fall without resisting. Lower the weight, don't drop it.

The military press, presented earlier in the discussion of exercises on arm extension, is also good for the deltoids. Stand with your feet flat and shoulder-width apart. Start by holding the bar just under the chin, then press it upward. Watch for extra motions of the leg and back that help do the work and prevent isolation.

Isotonic machines — Again, there are only slight differences in the exercises performed with barbells and dumbbells and those

Lateral Arm Raise (Front)

Hold the dumbbells in front of you to emphasize the front part of the deltoid.

Use an overhand grip.

Raise the dumbbells over your head.

with isotonic machines. Nautilus double arm machines mimic lateral raises. Military presses can be performed at appropriate stations on most isotonic setups.

Nautilus Double Arm Machine (Deltoid)

Nautilus double-arm machines duplicate lateral raises.

With hands on the grips, lift the weights upward.

Lower the weights slowly and gradually.

Vertical Adduction

Three major muscle groups are involved in the motion of pulling the arms down: the lattissimus dorsi (lats) and teres major in the back, and the part of the pectoralis major that attaches to the chest bone and upper arm. Use the chest exercises to strengthen those muscles. We will consider the back muscles here.

Isotonic machines — Almost all machine groups have a lat station. The best exercise for the lats is the lat pulldown.

Facing away from the machine, hold the bar at extreme ends with an overhand grip. With arms extended, kneel directly below the center of the bar. Pull the bar down until it touches the back of your neck.

Lat Pull Down

Kneel while doing the lat pull down on the Universal machine.

Bring the bar down behind your neck.

Use an overhand grip.

Be careful not to bend your hips and back to help accelerate the weights. If you are using a heavy weight, you may find that it pulls you off the floor. If this occurs, sit cross-legged on the floor with one or two 25-pound barbell weights on your lap.

An alternate exercise at the station is the straight-arm pull.

This time, stand facing the machine and grab the bar with an overhand grip. The hands should be about shoulder-width apart. Keeping your arms straight at the elbows, pull the bar down in an arc until it is close to your thighs. Lower the weight (raise the bar) at a slow and controlled rate.

No equipment — If a machine is not available, you can rely on wide-grip chin-ups. Use an overhand grip that is double your shoulder width. Pull yourself up to the bar, leaning your head forward so that you touch the back of your neck to the bar.

Wide Grip Chin-Ups for the Lats

Wide-grip chin-ups work the lats.

Use an overhand grip and pull your chin up to the bar.

Wide-grip chin-ups are very difficult.

Raising and Lowering Shoulder Blades — The lower trapezius is the primary muscle involved in depression of the shoulder blade. Exercises for it have been covered previously in suggestions for the horizontal arm abductors.

Elevating the shoulder blades is caused primarily by the pull of the upper part of the trapezius and the levator scapulae. Both attach to the neck: the trapezius attaches to the collarbone and the levator to the shoulder blade.

Using isotonic machines — The bench press station on weight machines can be used for shoulder shrugs. Shrugs are the best exercises for these muscles. Grab the bar with an overhand grip with the hands shoulder-width apart. Bring the bar to the starting position—legs and back straight and holding the bar in front of you. Then pull your shoulders upward.

Dumbbells or barbells — The technique for barbells is the same as that for weight machines. When using dumbbells, hold them with an overhand grip directly at your sides. Raise your shoulders together or alternately. Think of touching your ears with your shoulders.

It is helpful to do this exercise in front of a mirror. The most common error is bending the elbows, which allows the arm flexors to help. If you find the motion awkward, start with little or no weight.

Shoulder Shrugs

Shoulder shrugs can be done with dumb-bells or with a barbell.

Raise your shoulders together when using a barbell.

THE FOOT

The foot moves around the ankle joint in two different planes. In the first, it moves up and down relative to the lower leg. Upward movement by the toes is called dorsi flexion and is done by the muscles in the front of the lower leg. Lack of development of these muscles can lead to shinsplints.

The opposite muscle groups, which move the toes down, are the gastrocnemius and soleus, commonly known as the calf muscles. These are frequently much stronger than their shin counterparts and the resulting muscle imbalance can create injury problems for runners.

Motions in the second (horizontal) plane are called eversion when the outside of the foot is rotated upward and inversion when it is rotated downward. These muscles get little or no exercise in most programs, which is unfortunate, because they play a significant role in the prevention of ankle sprains.

Exercises for the muscles that control the foot do not require a high level of cardiovascular effort. Nonetheless, for a balanced strength workout they need to be included in many exercise programs. For aerobic strength training you can use these exercises during a brief rest between strenuous exercises or you can do them after you complete the AST workout.

Ankle Extension — The calf muscles pull the heel up, and the toes move down in this motion. Exercises are easily accomplished.

Isotonic machines — Use the leg press station of the exercise machine. Press the pedals forward so your legs are straight. Then slip your feet down so that the balls of your feet are supporting the weight. Flex your toes up and down.

No equipment — Standing on a step or a solid board, move your feet to the rear so that only the balls of your feet are on it. Hold onto something for stability. Raise up on your toes, then lower yourself to a comfortable position. Don't lower beyond a comfortable position.

Dumbbells — You can increase the resistance provided by the no-equipment toe raises by doing them on one leg at a time or by holding a dumbbell in the hand on the side of the exercise. The other hand is used for stability.

It is very important to adequately stretch both the calf muscles and Achilles tendon after exercising them. Injuries to the Achilles are common because of tightness of the calf muscles.

Calf Raises Using the Leg Press Station

Calf raises can be done on a Universal machine leg press station.

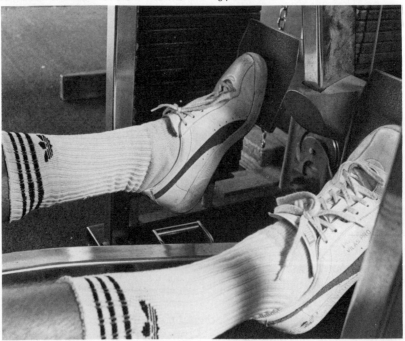

Support the pedals from the balls of your feet. Flex your toes.

cont'd next page

Calf Raises Using the Leg Press Station (cont'd)

Keep your legs straight while sitting at the station.

Calf Raises

Calf raises can be done using only a board.

Push up from the board. The balls of your feet should be over the board.

Ankle Flexion — Weakness of the dorsi flexion muscles that bring the toes up, along with a lack of flexibility, contribute heavily to shin splints.

Ankle weights or iron boot — In order to strengthen the flexion muscles, fasten an ankle weight around the ball of one foot. Put the heel on the edge of a step or board so that the foot can move freely up and down. Raise and lower the weight. If you have access to an iron boot, use it instead of ankle weights.

No equipment — This exercise does not require equipment, but does take a partner. Sit on the floor with your legs straight out in front. Your partner places the palm of one hand over the toes of one of your feet and puts his other hand cupped beneath the heel of that foot. Pull your toes upward against his resistance.

Ankle Eversion — Most ankle sprains are inversions. That is, the foot twists down to the outside. If the muscles that pull the outside of the foot up (eversion) are strong enough to withstand a sideways twist, ankle sprains can be prevented.

Isotonic or ankle exercise machines — Physical therapy departments in hospitals have ankle exercise machines. If you have access to one, use it for all your ankle exercises. It consists of a metal shoe to which you strap your foot. The shoe rotates in either the flexion-extension or eversion-inversion planes.

Without equipment, the recommended exercise is ankle roll-overs. Stand in front of the military press station of a weight machine or in front of a tall bureau. Put your hands and forearms on the bar to support some of your weight. Put your feet close together and rotate them outward over the outer edge of each foot. Continue the rotation as far as is comfortable, then return to a normal standing position. Repeat fifteen to twenty times. To increase resistance, exercise just one ankle at a time with your full body weight or hold weights in your hands.

Another variation requires a partner. Lie on the floor on your back with your legs straight in front of you. The partner puts one hand on the outside of your foot. The other goes under your heel. Rotate your toes to the outside, while he resists. At the greatest point of contraction, have him overcome your resistance, pushing your toes back to the inside. Then have him decrease the resistance just enough so you can rotate your toes again to the outside.

Elastic bands can be used instead of a partner. Cut strips from a bicycle inner tube and tie the ends to make a band that is big enough so both feet can fit inside when it is not stretched. From a

Ankle Flexion or Shin Strengtheners

Flexion muscles are strengthened if you place a weight over your foot and flex upward.

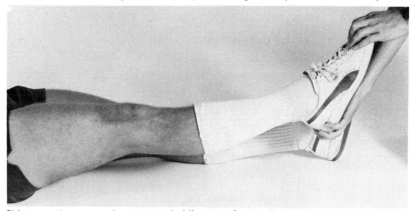

Shin strengtheners require a partner holding your foot at the toes.

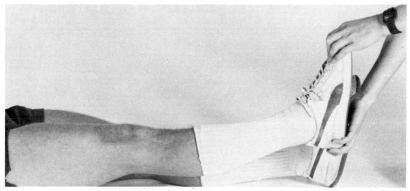

Pull your toes upward and back against his resistance.

Inward Ankle Rotation

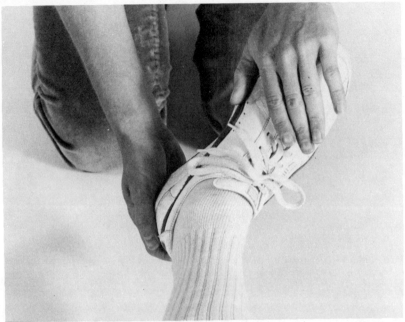

Inward ankle rotation is similar to outward rotation.

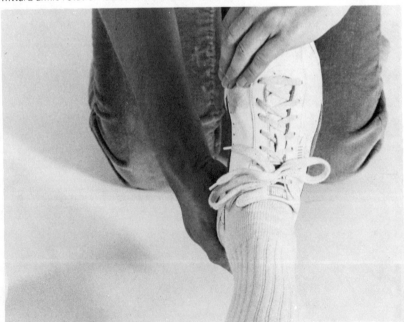

In this case, rotate against resistance inward.

Outward Ankle Rotation

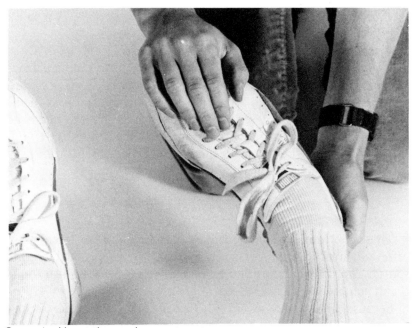

Outward ankle rotation requires a partner, too.

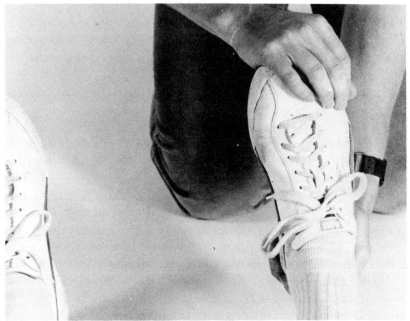

Rotate your toes to the outside, while he resists.

sitting position with straight legs and with the band around your feet below the toes, rotate both feet to the outside while keeping your heels in place.

Ankle Inversion — These muscles do not need as much work as the eversion group; however, you can exercise them to keep a balance between antagonistic muscles.

No equipment — Using a partner and similar position as in the eversion exercises just described, have the partner place one hand on the inside of your foot and the other beneath it. Rotate your foot inward against resistance, then have him push your foot back in the other direction.

WRIST AND HAND

These motions are controlled by a complex set of twenty-five different muscle groups. They are especially important in racket sports. The same muscles that extend and flex the wrist also rotate it and control the grip.

Because these exercises do not heavily tax your cardiovascular system, you may want to do them after finishing your regular aerobic strength training. As an alternative, use them to catch your breath in the middle of a circuit.

Wrist Extension — The motion extends the back of the hand up and toward the forearm. It is controlled by muscles attached to the forearm and bones in the hand.

Barbells, weights — Reverse wrist curls provide good development. Using an overhand grip, grab a barbell at shoulder width. Use little or no weight. Rest the forearms on the thighs and let the wrists extend beyond the knees. Flex your wrists down as far as they will go, then back up as far as possible. Watch your forearms and make sure they do not move.

An alternate exercise is the reverse wrist roll-up. Tie a piece of rope through a half-inch dowel and tie the other end to a five-pound weight. Hold the dowel in front of you with an overhand grip and roll the rope up around the dowel by flexing one wrist at a time. When this becomes easy, increase the weight.

No weights — Make a fist with the wrist to be exercised. Cup your other hand over it. Then flex your fist back and forth while opposing the extensor motion with a cupped hand.

Reverse Wrist Curls

For reverse wrist curls, use an overhand grip.

Rest the forearms on the thighs. Flex your wrists as far up as they will go. Use a light weight.

Reverse Wrist Roll Ups

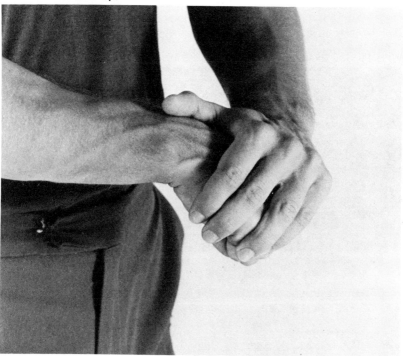

Reverse wrist roll ups call for making a fist, then resisting the extensor motion.

Wrist Flexion — These muscles pull the wrist down, toward the underside of the arm.

Barbells, weights — Wrist curls are the most effective exercises for this group. Sit on a chair and grab a barbell with an underhand grip, shoulder width. Rest the back of the forearm along the thighs with wrists extended. Flex the wrists up and down. Since these muscles are usually stronger than the extensors, you can probably

Wrist Curls

Use an underhand grip for standard wrist curls.

You can probably use more weight than for reverse wrist curls.

Wrist Flexion Exercise

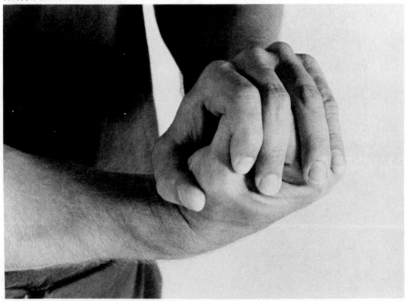
In this wrist flexion exercise, resist the flexing motion.

Newspaper Wad

Wadding a sheet of newspaper works the wrist muscles.

Start with one corner of a full page in your grip.

Reverse Grip Exercise

Place the palm of the other hand over the clenched fingers.

A reverse grip exercise calls for making a fist and resisting the motion of extending the fingers.

use more weight. You can also do the wrist roll-ups for flexors. Simply use an underhand grip instead of an overhand grip.

No weights — As in the exercise for the extensors, place a fist in a cupped hand. This time oppose the flexing motion.

Grip — A strong grip is important in many sport activities. Weakness here frequently does not manifest itself until muscles tire late in a contest.

Using grip devises — Most sporting goods stores have a variety of mechanical devices for improving grip. The important thing to remember is to buy one that is stiff enough to sufficiently overload your muscles. If you can do twenty repetitions in the store, it's probably too soft.

No equipment — One simple exercise is to wad a sheet of newspaper. Place one corner of a full page in your grip. Without help from the other hand, wad up the entire page.

An exercise for finger extension is to make a fist with one hand and place the palm of the other hand over the clenched fingers. Open the fist to full extension while opposing with the closed hand.

THE HEAD

Exercises for the neck muscles that move the head are very important to preventing injuries in contact sports. Using weights requires a head harness or a neck machine. The harness wraps around the head and attaches to a barbell weight. Nautilus has a four-way neck machine that is very good.

Neck Extensions — This movement is the motion of pulling the head up and to the rear.

Weights or machines — Use a 2.5- or 5-pound weight on a head harness. Stand with your feet a little closer than shoulder width and knees flexed. Bend forward at the waist, placing hands on your thighs. Pull the weight up as far as possible and lower it until neck is in horizontal position.

No equipment — The neck pulldown is done by locking your fingers behind your head as if you were going to do sit-ups. Pull your head down until your chin touches your chest, while opposing this motion with your neck. Then let your neck muscles pull the head back up. Use light resistance for five to ten reps initially.

Nautilus Four-Way Neck Machine

The Nautilus four-way neck machine is very good.

cont'd next page

Nautilus Four-Way Neck Machine (cont'd)

You can work the back, front and sides of your neck.

cont'd next page

Nautilus Four-Way Neck Machine (cont'd)

Be sure to go through the full range of motion on the machine.

cont'd next page

Nautilus Four-Way Neck Machine (cont'd)

Assume the four positions, as shown.

Neck Pull Down

For the neck pulldown lock your fingers behind your head.

Head Push-Up

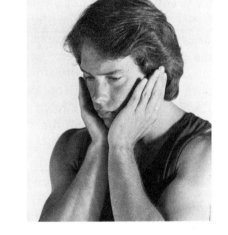

To do a head push-up, put your hands beneath your chin.

Neck Flexion — Flexing the neck is pulling the head forward and down.

Weights or machines — To exercise flexors, simply reverse the two exercises for the extensors.

With the head harness, lie on your back on a bench. Extend your head and neck beyond the edge of the bench and attach a harness with five pounds or less. Start with your neck horizontal and pull it up until your chin touches your chest. Then lower it back to the starting position.

No equipment — The head push-up is accomplished by placing both hands beneath the chin. Push up with your hands while re-sisting with your neck flexors. When your head is as far back as is comfortable, reduce the force of your arms and move your head forward and down. Again, do five to ten reps with light resistance.

STRETCHING OUT

Your aerobic strength training program should be complemented with a stretching program. Increased flexibility and the prevention of injuries are the primary benefits of this program. A secondary benefit is increasing the efficiency with which you can perform the workouts.

The following are some stretches suggested specifically for the muscle groups as defined in this chapter. See Chapter 2 for general rules on stretching.

For Leg Extensors (quadriceps) — Stand with one hand against a wall for support. Grab the toes of one foot with the other hand and gently pull the toes up toward your butt. Hold the position for twenty seconds, then switch sides.

For Leg Flexors (hamstrings) — Sit on the floor with your legs straight at the knee and spread at right angles to each other. Bend the right leg up and place the sole of your right foot alongside the left knee. Then bend forward and reach toward your left foot with both hands. Point the toes of your left foot up, not to the side. Reach a comfortable stretch position and hold it for twenty seconds, then relax. Repeat the stretch on the opposite leg.

For Hip Extensors (gluteus maximus) — While standing, bend one leg and grab it with both hands just below the knee. Pull the knee up toward your chest and hold until you feel the stretch in your buttocks.

For Upper Leg Flexion (hip flexors) — Start in a kneeling position. Put your right foot on the floor in front of you and the left knee on the ground as far back as possible. Lean forward without moving either the right or left foot and hold the stretch. Repeat on the other leg.

For Upper Leg Abduction — Lie on your back with your knees bent and put your hands behind your head. Cross one leg over the opposite knee and use it to pull the second leg toward the floor. Keep the shoulders squarely on the floor.

For Upper Leg Adduction — Start in a sitting position with your knees bent and the soles of your feet together. Hold onto your toes with your hands and bend forward. Ideally, touch the floor with your nose, but stop when you reach a comfortable stretch.

Quadriceps Stretch

Pull your toes toward your butt in the leg extensor (quadriceps) stretch.

Hamstring Stretch

Work one leg at a time in the leg flexor (hamstring) stretch.

Hip Extensor Stretch

The hip extensor stretch affects the gluteus maximus.

Hip Flexor Stretch

Lean forward in the hip flexor stretch.

Leg Abductor Stretch

Use one leg to pull the other leg to the floor in the leg abductor stretch.

Groin Stretch

The groin stretch is good for upper leg adduction.

For Trunk Extension — Toe touches are effective. Spread feet shoulder-width apart, bend at the waist and reach for your toes. You don't have to reach them, just get a good stretch. Another method starts from a cross-legged sitting position. Bend forward and try to touch your head on the floor.

For Trunk Flexion (abdominals) — Lie on the floor on your back. Stretch your arms out over your head and your toes in the opposite direction. This will stretch several other muscles besides the abdominals.

For Lower Arm Extensors (triceps) — Place the palm of one hand flat on the opposite shoulder blade, passing the bent arm behind your head. With your free hand, pull the elbow downward into a stretch.

For Lower Arm Flexors (biceps) — Stand near a doorway or a post. Grab the doorway or post with one hand. Twist your body

Toe Touches

Crossed-leg toe touches are effective for trunk extension.

Body Stretch

The full-body stretch affects muscles besides the abdominals.

Triceps Stretch

The triceps stretch works the lower arm extensors.

away from the arm so that it is fully extended at the elbow. Continue until you find a comfortable stretch.

For Horizontal Arm Abductors (trapezius) — Stand in a doorway or near a post. Grab the post or doorway and rotate your body out, toward the arm, until you feel the stretch.

For Horizontal Arm Adductors (pectorals, deltoids) — The best stretch requires a partner. Kneel with your hands behind your head. Have your partner come up behind and place his arms in front of your elbows. He grasps his hands behind your back and then gently pulls backward on your elbows.

Without a partner, grab a towel behind your head. Pull it up, over your head and as far back as is comfortable. Try a variety of positions to see which gives you the best stretch sensation.

Chest Stretch

The chest stretch calls for using a towel. Hold it behind your head.

Upper Trapezius Stretch

For the upper trapezius stretch, push your knee against your arms.

For Vertical Arm Abductors (deltoids) — Find a lat station on an isotonic setup or a fence or bar that is strong and about shoulder high. Spread your arms and hold the bar with an overhand grip. Let your upper body go limp, supported by legs and arms. Moving from side to side will stretch various sets of muscles.

For Vertical Arm Adductors (lattisimus dorsi, teres major) — Hanging from a high bar is a good stretch for the vertical adductors. Use an overhand grip on a bar that is high enough so your feet will not touch the ground.

For Raising/Lowering Shoulders (trapezius, levator scapulae) — With your back against a wall, rest your butt on the wall and clasp your fingers together around one knee. Push your knee downward, pulling your arms.

For Ankle Extension (calf muscles, gastrocnemius and soleus) — Place one foot near a wall or post and the other about two feet back. Put your hands on the wall for support. Keep the rear leg straight and the front leg bent and lean forward. You should feel a stretch in the calf. If not, move the rear leg farther away from the wall. To stretch the Achilles tendon, repeat the movement, but bend the rear leg at the knee. Switch legs.

Shin Muscles Stretch

Keep the rear leg straight in the shin muscles stretch.

For Ankle Flexion (shins) — Lie stomach-down on the floor. Toes should touch the floor and be pointing away from you. Slowly do a push-up to the fully extended position. Allow your hips to fall and arch your back, which will increase the intensity of the stretch.

For Wrist Muscles — Stand near a wall and place your hands flat on it, about chest-high with the fingers up. Lean forward. To increase the stretch, move the hands farther down the wall. To stretch the opposing group, form a fist and pull it inward with your other hand. Apply tension to one knuckle at a time to accentuate the stretch in different muscles.

Wrist Stretch

For the wrist stretch, place your hands flat on a wall. Lean forward.

For Neck Muscles — Roll your neck. Start by holding it back as far as comfortable, then slowly rotate to one side. When it is tilted forward, hold it in that stretched position and then continue. After a few slow rotations, reverse direction.

Neck Roll Stretch

Start the neck roll stretch with your neck back.

cont'd next page

Neck Roll Stretch (cont'd)

Slowly rotate your neck to one side.

Neck Roll Stretch (cont'd)

When the neck is tilted forward, hold it in a stretch position.

cont'd next page

Neck Roll Stretch (cont'd)

After a few slow rotations, reverse direction.

6

Circuit Training

Many weightlifters believe that cardiovascular fitness is obtained through general weight training. It's just not so. The very nature of the exercise—sudden bursts of effort pushing medium to heavy resistance—is not conducive to an aerobic training effect.

However, application of an interval concept to weight training will allow you to turn conventional lifting methods into aerobic training. As indicated previously, this technique allows you to develop a program with a mix of aerobic and anaerobic training.

We prefer the use of weights for "indoor" circuit training, since with them it is possible to isolate and quickly work out specific muscle groups. However, weight equipment is not necessary for circuit training. Indoor and outdoor fitness trails utilize the same principles, though they are timed in a different manner. England's mile world-record holder, Sebastian Coe, uses a circuit training program, one that does not involve weights.

We will discuss non-weight programs later, but initially will deal with the use of weights for the strength training exercises of the preceeding chapter.

TECHNIQUES OF CIRCUIT WEIGHT TRAINING

There are two variable elements of the program: a timing method and weight equipment.

Aerobic strength training, with a fixed exercise time, requires either someone timing the participants in the program or an automatic timing system.

In programs developed at the Boulder, Colorado, YMCA, we found that a cassette recorder using a timed tape is an excellent tool. The tape can provide entertaining music as well as the essential time commands that control the rotation of participants.

Choice of time is the most important element in creation of a circuit. We recommend a base of thirty seconds—that is, each exercise will be started on the half-minute. Some other programs call for a forty-five-second exercise base with rest periods of less than a minute.

How long you exercise during each thirty-second period is determined by your fitness level. You might exercise for ten, fifteen or twenty seconds, depending on your current condition. The timer, or timing tape, calls out the time at each of these intervals.

After you have finished your exercise period, you use the remainder of the thirty-second period to get to the next exercise station and prepare for the next exercise.

We recommend the thirty-second base as an optimum for general conditioning programs. Using twenty seconds for exercise and ten seconds to change stations allows you to get in the ideal number of repetitions, between eight and fifteen.

There are instances in which you may wish to alter the base rate of thirty seconds, particularly if you are trying to match training to your particular sport. A sprinter may want to train in ten- to twelve-second bursts if he is running 100-meter sprints during the track season. A soccer player may use the full twenty seconds with lighter weights, thus maximizing the number of repetitions and the endurance development.

Aerobic weight training is designed to elevate the heart rate and keep it elevated for a long time (more than ten minutes). Using longer time bases than the thirty- to forty-five-second range could allow your cardiovascular work level to drop below that needed for optimum training effects.

You may wish to use heart rate monitoring, in addition to the timing system to ensure that you are getting an optimum workout. Monitor your heart rate during exercise and compare it with the rate during other times of the day. A healthy heart should be able to respond to demands rapidly, and return rapidly to a normal rate. Take your pulse right after exercising, then continue to take it at minute intervals afterward, to see how quickly it returns to a resting level. It should drop below one-hundred beats per minute within three minutes of finishing exercising. It should also drop to within five beats per minute of your pre-exercise pulse in half an hour. During interval training for athletes age eighteen to thirty, the heart rate should approach a maximum in the range of 180 beats a minute, then return to approximately 120 beats a minute during the rest interval. If it does not recover to this 120 - 130 beat range, the interval has been too long or too strenuous. You can adjust this figure according to your current age and maximum pulse rates by using the pulse rate tables presented in Chapter 2.

When you're just starting out, it's best to use the ten-second exercise duration (in a thirty-second program) until you feel comfortable exercising through three full sets. Add time increments of five seconds to the third set of exercises, a few exercises at each workout. When the third set is at the higher exercise rate, gradually increase the time in the preceding sets. The maximum advisable exercise time is twenty seconds, using the thirty-second base.

In Chapter 3 we discussed how to choose weights for strength exercise. Basically, the concept is to maximize the total work (force x distance x number of repetitions) done by selecting an optimum weight.

You will know when you should change the weight on each exercise. If your muscles tire before the time limit is reached on a set, decrease the weight. On the other hand, if you reach the time limit and are still pumping strongly, increase the weight. Aim to reach muscle fatigue at the end of the set.

THE EQUIPMENT AND ROUTINE

Any isotonic or isokinetic exercise can be incorporated into this aerobic system. You can use any of the exercises that you would in conventional weight training.

There are usually between eight and sixteen exercises in each circuit, or set. Usually there are three circuits per workout. You can use cardiovascular exercises along with strength exercises within the circuit. Running in place, pedaling a stationary bicycle or doing jumping jacks can be done for a minute or more between circuits or in place of a strength exercise.

Weight machines are quite useful in that you can quickly change the weights for each exercise within the few seconds allowed between exercises. However, many machines are not well-adapted to the rapid changes required in the circuit training schedule. And machines that have restraining straps or complicated entry design, make the transition difficult in a thirty-second base program.

The order in which you do your exercises is dependent primarily on the facility and equipment you are using, as well as the size of the training group. Ideally, the facility should have a complete set of equipment, including a multi-station gym with the following systems:

bench press
military press
back extension
rows/curls
high lats
leg press
sit-up board,
a leg machine for:

       leg extension
       leg flexion

chinning bar
barbells
dumbbells
exercise bike
exercise step
neck harness
ankle weights or iron boots
inclined board.

Barbells and dumbbells give you the ability to exercise almost any muscle in any particular motion you desire. The problem with using them is the time needed to change the weights. Dumbbells should be of one-piece construction and therefore you need a set of them from five pounds to fifty pounds in five-pound increments.

Two or three barbells usually suffice, even for a group workout with people of varying strengths. Set the bars up before starting to exercise and do not try to change the weights during the workout. However, do have each person check the collars before they pick up a bar. Loose collars can mean sore toes.

All of this equipment should be located in a large room. It must be big enough so that several people working out do not interfere with one another. Also it should be well-ventilated, well-lighted and carpeted.

Few facilities can meet the standards of the previously described ideal facility. If you find one that meets most of them and is convenient for you, use it.

Since there's only a short time between exercises, it's helpful to have the stations close together and laid out to minimize traffic problems. When you have a dozen or more people hurrying from exercise to exercise, in a limited space, things can get hectic, so simple layouts are better. Try to keep moving in one direction, clockwise or counterclockwise around the room.

Although working a large group may seem to be a hassle, there are benefits. Even when using weight machines, assistance is often needed in setting weights and equipment. People working out can help each other, but additional assistance can make the workout more efficient. You might have a group split into two: one group sets weights while the other exercises.

Exercise form is of particular importance in the circuit training sequence. When you're tired and moving quickly, there's a danger of sacrificing form for speed. Concentrate on moving only the muscles involved in the exercise. Ask the timer or an observer to watch your form for excess motion. Remember, doing the exercise with improper form yields poor strength gains and may result in injury.

There are other ways to prevent injury and help develop good form. Make sure that you have stretched and thoroughly warmed up before starting. A good method of warming up is to go to each station before the workout starts and do several repetitions, using weights lighter than normal or no weight at all.

While exercising, have the timer call "ready" one second before "go" to tell you when to take the strain. This will allow you to gradually move the weight to the starting position, rather than jerking it up.

TESTING

Since circuit training is a combination of strength training and cardiovascular training, you may want to test each element separately.

Using any of the aerobic tests included in Chapter 2, such as Cooper's twelve-minute test, can give you an indication of your cardiovascular development.

For measuring gains in strength, you might want to do a two-minute exercise test in three exercises, for example the bench press, sit-ups and leg press. Do as many repetitions as you can in the two minutes—using weights lighter than you use during normal training. Record the weights and reps accomplished so you can compare with future results.

You can also keep an ongoing record of the repetitions you do for each exercise in a workout. In order to compare workout efforts when you have changed resistance, multiply the weight used by the number of repetitions. This gives you the value of work performed.

OF INTEREST TO RUNNERS: THE COE CIRCUIT

As indicated previously, the exercise circuit does not have to be limited strictly to weights or weight machines, particularly not when specific training in a sport or certain events is involved.

An excellent example of this concept is the circuit training program used by Britain's Sebastian Coe. Coe and countryman Steve Ovett have been the two most dominating middle-distance runners in the world for the last few years. Coe has now utilized various forms of circuit training for the last five years.

Coe's off-season program is performed indoors, as are many sport programs in England, where harsh winters force athletes to substitute circuit training for outdoor training. Coe uses circuit training to augment his training regimes, running (of course), stretching sessions and sprint drills.

Coe's circuit is performed indoors, but it's again important to note the difference in terminology between indoor and outdoor circuits. The differentiation between the two is only the timing method. For most indoor circuits a certain amount of time is allowed at each exercise station. You attempt to maximize repetitions. Outdoor circuits require a fixed number of repetitions at each station, which the participants try to perform as quickly as possible before moving. The objective outdoors is to minimize the total time required.

Coe's program includes a variety of exercises. Rope climbs, dips and inclined push-ups help build the upper chest and back muscles. While not of prime importance to running, he includes them to maintain general conditioning.

Leg speed is developed through reverse splits, depth jumps, beam jumps, continuous step-ups and low thrusts. Bounding, a slowed down and exaggerated form of running, is added to the circuit to help in development.

Back extension strengthens the lower back muscles, and leg raises strengthen hip flexors. Sit-ups are done to help develop stomach muscles.

A Coe circuit might follow this order:

1. Rope Climb (fifteen feet).

2. Reverse Splits. With one foot well to the front and the other well to the rear, he then jumps up, changing the position of his legs rapidly.

3. Beam Jumps. Holding onto a beam of demanding height, he drops to the floor and immediately tries to bounce back up to the starting position.

4. Back Extensions.

5. Step-Ups. He completes the workout for one leg before starting on the other.

6. Dips.

7. Depth Jumps. Coe uses three boxes, spaced far enough apart so he can land between them. He jumps with both feet to the top of one box, then down to the space between, then back to the top of the second box. After finishing the third box, he returns to the first box and repeats the exercise.

8. Inclined Push-Ups (with feet elevated).

9. Low Thrusts. From a sprinter's position, with one leg back and one forward, he drives forward off the front foot, covering as much ground as possible before landing in the starting position with legs reversed.

10. Leg Raises (hanging from bar).

11. Sit-Ups (knees bent).

12. Bounding. The knees are picked up higher and held up longer than in actual running.

13. Burpees. From a position similar to push-ups, spring both legs forward close to the hands. Then leap up, drop down and drive the feet backward to the starting position.

Coe's warm-up routine includes one restricted trip through the circuit. He does two complete laps of the circuit, spending thirty seconds on each exercise. Fifteen seconds are allowed between exercises.

The physical gains in this program and other circuits could probably be achieved in other ways. But the program is quick, complete and convenient and should be an efficient conditioning method for almost any athlete.

BENEFITS OF CIRCUIT TRAINING

In recent years a number of experiments have been conducted to assess the routine of circuit training. It is difficult to compare the results of one study with another since they use different exercises and timing sequences. However, some fairly consistent results have emerged from these studies.

The studies have shown that circuit training increases strength, decreases body fat and improves cardiovascular conditioning. These fitness improvements typically have been produced with three workouts a week, each taking only twenty-five to thirty minutes.

The improvements in cardiovascular conditioning relative to strength gains depend on the direction of the workout and the length of time allowed between sets and between circuits. Unfortunately, sufficient testing has not been done to know the optimum training techniques.

PART THREE

THE APPLICATIONS

7

Fitness Trail Running

Outdoor curcuit training courses have been used for many years in fitness and conditioning classes in Europe but only recently became popular here. Today, fitness tails can be found throughout the country under a number of different names and forms. The first, and probably still most popular circuits were brought to this country in the early 1970s by Parcourse Ltd.

An outdoor circuit training course (OCTC) consists of any number of exercise stations placed along a running path. The stations are usually at least one-hundred yards (but not more than three-hundred yards) apart and the circuit is ideally suited for parks or recreation facilities. You may run or walk from station to station, doing a specific number of reps for each exercise at each stop.

The popularity of the OCTC owes much to the running boom, because it is possible to get a strength workout as part of your daily run. Fitness trails can also be set up inside a gymnasium. Chin-ups, push-ups, vaulting, step-ups, and other exercises can be included in such an indoor circuit, allowing you to run between the widely spaced equipment.

On most fitness trails produced commercially, the runner selects one of three intensity levels for the workout. At each station along the way, the number of repetitions necessary for that intensity level is indicated. You can start out at the easiest level and work your way to the hardest. You are also competing on a different level by trying to reduce the elapsed time needed to cover the course.

Most outdoor circuits are laid out along a 1-1.5-mile running path and include twelve to twenty exercise stations. They take approximately twelve to twenty minutes to complete, providing an intense but short workout. To add more endurance training just run the course more than once. You might also do the course twice, but insert one run in between, in which you run only. On these expanded workouts you will probably want to drop down one level of intensity.

You should stretch before and after running the fitness trail. A short jog or some skipping is also suggested before beginning.

Instructional signs are prevalent at the start of the course and at each exercise station. Move at a comfortable pace. Doing the exercises will raise your heart rate considerably, while a slow, easy run between exercises allows it to return to a manageable rate. This sort of workout gives both aerobic and anaerobic training benefits.

BUILDING YOUR OWN

If you do not live in a community that provides such a fitness trail, or are part of a group that is interested in adding a trail in your community, there are several reasons to consider building your own fitness trail, the first being cost. Ordering a ready-made course from manufacturers is expensive. Contact area manufacturers to get price quotes. Another is the diversity you can build into your trail that might not be included in some commercial versions.

The layout of your course will depend on the space and area available. An ideal location is along a closed-loop running path. There are certain advantages to an out-and-back set-up but certainly the OCTC should be near a natural meeting ground for runners, such as a track or popular park.

The course should be 1-1.5 miles long and the spacing of exercise stations is dictated by the terrain, but generally they should be equidistant. The exercises should also be arranged so that you are not exercising similar muscle groups on adjacent stations.

The intensity of exercise on the course should build gradually at the start and tapered off at the end. The tempo of the course can be established by varying how a user travels from one station to another. For example, we have had people run backward to the first station. This forces them to start more slowly than running forward would. Also, it can be fun to run backward. Skipping between stations would also be good for slowing your progress between stations. Specify that the knees be brought up high during skipping; this action is a good warm-up exercise.

The main expense for an outdoor circuit is instructional signs. They need not be fancy, though. Simple and durable signs will do. Hand-painted or wood-routed signs can do as good a job as the more expensive and fancier manufactured versions.

Perhaps the most serious drawback of manufactured courses is that they mix stretching with strength-building exercises. Stretching should be done before and after the workout, not in the middle of it. The stretching exercises included in the course are usually too few, and they take away potential stations for strength development.

If you are building your own course, we suggest building a stretching area near the start and finish. In the OCTC use at least ten exercises for strength. Wherever possible use each station for two exercises. This reduces your materials and the time needed for building and installation. A half-mile track that can be run twice or an out-and-back trail allows you to do this.

You have a variety of exercises to choose from. Here are some of the most popular, which you will probably encounter on many commercial fitness trails. Whenever possible, design one piece of equipment for more than one exercise.

CHIN-UP STATION

If you are going to include a ladder walk station in your program, it can also be used for chin-ups. If not, you need to consider the average height of those who will be using your chin-up station.

A simple station consists of four bars of different heights supported by four 4" x 6" posts set in a square. The bars should be one-inch galvanized pipe. The length of the vertical posts is equal to the tallest bar plus about 20 percent. The additional length is set in concrete below the ground. Add enough height so that those at each extreme of body height can hang with their feet a few inches off the ground.

Another exercise that can be done at this station is the knee raise. Hanging from the bar with feet and knees together, raise your knees to your chest, then lower again.

SIT-UP STATION

Sit-ups belong in every fitness program. The suggested design here is a sit-up board. Four boards are elevated at different angles, with their upper ends supported by posts. The different elevations give different levels of difficulty. Loops of rope are provided for securing the feet.

You can also use this station for doing leg raises and lateral leg raises. By reversing direction and using the rope for a hand hold, you can lift the legs on leg raises. Lateral raises can be done while lying on the side.

PUSH-UP STATION

Equipment for push-ups may seem unnecessary, but it does protect the hands during inclement weather. Also, it can be used for several other exercises.

A station can be constructed of galvanized pipe. Bars of three or more different heights should be included. The lowest difficulty push-ups are done with the hands on the tallest bar. The difficulty increases as the height is decreased. By putting your feet on the tallest bar and your hands on the ground you get even greater intensity.

The push-up station can also be used for reverse push-ups, done with your back to the bar and the feet in front. The back shuffle can also be done at the station. Grab the bar behind you while squatting in front of it. Then kick the feet outward, away from the bar, until they are fully extended, and bring them back together. Another exercise that can be done is the hip raise. In the same starting position as for the back shuffle, raise your hips as high as possible while contracting the stomach muscles. This is an excellent exercise for muscles in the back and posterior.

LADDER WALK

We're all familiar with the overhead climbing ladders on playgrounds. The same equipment can add a good exercise to an OCTC. The exercise works a variety of shoulder, back and arm muscles.

The ladder should be about eight feet above the ground and include at least ten rungs, spaced ten to twelve inches apart. The intensity of the exercise is determined by how far you travel along the ladder.

An even more basic piece of equipment is two parallel bars of ten-foot length. Instead of going rung to rung, you travel by sliding your hands along the pipe.

To start, jump up and grab the ladder or the bars with an overhand grip. Pull up until your arm and forearm are at a ninety-degree angle, then cross the ladder by alternating arms across. If you cannot hold the bent-arm position, do the exercise with straight arms.

PARALLEL BARS

There are many exercises that can be done on a parallel bar station, including a parallel bar walk. To do the walk you travel the length of the bars by supporting your weight on your arms and sliding your hands forward. Body dips, one of the most popular exercises for the triceps, can also be done at this station.

STEP-UP STATION

Bleachers make an ideal place to do these exercises. Or, you can easily build a step-up station using logs or 4" x 6" boards set in the ground. Make several steps at two- to three-inch intervals between twelve and twenty inches high. Step-ups should be done so that you change legs only once per set. An alternative exercise is running stairs. There are plenty in a sports stadium.

BALANCE BEAM

This is often used as the warm-down station on many circuits. It is a fun station, which focuses on coordination, rather than strength. Keep the beam close to the ground to minimize the chance of injury. A 4" x 6" board placed on edge makes a usable, sturdy beam. You can go forward or backward on the balance beam or go one direction and then the other. If you decide to travel in both directions, forward and backward, instruct those using the beam to always get on at one end and travel in the same direction. This is the most efficient way to use the beam. The best-designed balance beam is square, so that the start and end points are near each other.

SWIMMER'S KICK

The kick, good for muscles of the lower back and hips, is performed by bending forward so that your head and body are supported on the bench and your feet are on the ground. Hold on with your hands for support. Raise your legs together until they are horizontal, then lower them.

With a strap to hold your feet on the same bench, you can do back extensions. Lie on your stomach with your feet hooked under the strap and your waist on the edge of the table. Raise and lower your body from a ninety-degree angle (head almost on the ground) to horizontal (your back straight).

This station is rarely found outdoors but almost always is found in the weight room. The importance of strength in the back muscles, and the simplicity with which the station can be built, makes this station a top priority for an OCTC.

OTHER EXERCISES

You can devise stations for almost any strength exercise you want to include. Your choice of what exercises to include should be governed by what your training goals are and what outdoor facilities are available.

In general you should stay away from any equipment with moving parts or anything that can be easily damaged. Vandalism must be a consideration. Equipment that can be easily damaged will be. Also design all equipment to be as maintenance-free as possible. Use materials that do not require painting, such as galvanized nuts and bolts and weather-treated lumber.

REPETITION LEVELS

The number of repetitions you will be able to do on the course will be dictated by your own physical condition. Here are some suggested starting points for easy, intermediate and hard exercise levels. On commercial courses, you will be given similar numbers.

SUGGESTED REPETITIONS

Exercises	Easiest	Intermediate	Hardest
Chin-ups	2	6	10
Knee Raises	5	10	15
Sit-ups	10	15	20
Leg Raises	5	10	15
Lateral Leg Raises	10	15	20
Push-ups	10	15	25
Back Shuffle	10	15	20
Hip Raises	10	15	20
Ladder Walk	5 rungs	8 rungs	maximum
Parallel Bar Dips	1	3	5
Step-ups	10	20	30
Swimmer's Kick	10	20	30
Back Extensions	10	15	20
Jumping Jacks	20	35	50

You can make up your own par, in terms of repetitions, for a particular course. After all, par is merely a goal to shoot for. In setting par for other people, make sure the highest intensity levels are challenging and that the easiest can be done by the majority of users. Also, remember that you will not be able to do as many repetitions on an OCTC because of the strenuous running between stations. In a gym you can rest between exercises and therefore do more reps. The best way to determine par is to run the course several times yourself, and with several others, who are at varying levels of fitness.

RUNNING THE TRAIL

Weather, sports season and upcoming competition can all alter your schedule for using a fitness trail. Generally, three workouts a week should be maximum. If you are using indoor circuit training, outdoor circuits can be used as an alternative. For example, it can be substituted for indoor training one day a week or every two weeks.

You should have two primary goals in running the course, maximizing effort on the exercises while minimizing the time it takes to complete the circuit. Keep records of both elapsed time and repetitions accomplished, or intensity level.

Even if you designed the course and trail, you probably will have no idea just how difficult it is. Take a few trial runs when you are just becoming acquainted with a course so that you can estimate its difficulty. Do not try to run a course with maximum effort until you know how hard it is relative to your condition.

One of the training benefits of outdoor circuit running is the potential to increase anaerobic capacity. In running one of these courses, be aware that you can quickly deplete your anaerobic reserve. Pace yourself so that you do not reach a state of anaerobic depletion before finishing.

Recording the time it takes to run the course if you pursue it as a regular training tool can be very valuable. Records provide an accurate measure of overall fitness and will give a good indication of your fitness development.

8

General Fitness

Aerobic stength training programs are ideal for general fitness. The combination of strength and cardiovascular development, when coupled with a stretching-flexibility program, conforms to the proper means of attaining fitness. Few programs can fulfill the requirements of fitness as well and with such little time involvement.

Training benefits of aerobic strength workouts are only obtained through hard work during the relatively short exercise periods. Your improvements will be directly correlated with your efforts and their consistency.

Because aerobic strength workouts are short, you should complement them with longer-duration aerobic, or long slow distance training. Complementary programs, such as running or cycling, build cardiovascular endurance and some strength in a few muscles. But by themselves they do not meet the requirements of a total fitness program. When integrated with aerobic strength training, you get a complete program.

In designing a fitness-orientated aerobic strength program you should take into account what other training you will be doing. A person who puts in lots of miles running or bicycling may do only a few leg exercises. On the other hand, he may want to build strength in the quadriceps by including leg extensions.

Generally, a fitness program should contain exercises for all the major muscle groups. Of prime importance are muscles of the stomach and back. Next are the extensors and flexors of the legs and arms and other muscles of the shoulders.

You cannot adequately exercise all the muscles on the body or even all the muscle groups. There are just too many—you would be exhausted before you finished even part of a workout. Thus, you must choose which ones are most important to you.

The selection of exercises and the order in which they appear in a circuit are controlled by the facilities available. For aerobic strength workouts in a weight room, make the sequence as simple as possible. Keep everyone moving in the same direction and space adjacent exercises as closely as possible. For circuit training (whether done outdoors or indoors in a gym) spread the equipment as widely as possible, to allow for a long run between exercises. Try to keep the movement directions as simple as possible.

When starting your program, use eight to ten exercises in the circuit. Later, when you have grown accustomed to the workouts, you can expand them to include as many exercises as you wish. However, we suggest you do not have more than sixteen exercises. If you have more exercises you want to include, replace some of the sixteen exercises with others, either on alternate days or alternate circuits on each day.

On a piece of paper write the exercises of your program, the order in which they are to be done, and the weight to be used. Keep this with you for the first few workouts. Training sessions are hectic and as you tire, you are more likely to forget your program. If several people are working out together, they can help each other by giving the correct order of exercises as well as by setting some of the weights. On the leg press station of Universal multi-station units, for example, the chair you sit in is opposite the weights, where the adjustment key is located. If you use this multi-station equipment you can space participants so that someone is always available to change weight settings for another.

Go slowly at first. Many people push themselves too hard at their first workout and then never return. If you are serious about your commitment to fitness, you will be working out for years, so there's no reason in trying to meet all your fitness goals the first workout.

There are many programs for aerobic strength training, some of which will be described here.

THE BOULDER CIRCUIT

The Boulder Circuit was developed at the YMCA in Boulder, Colorado. The program appeals to people with a wide variety of sports interest and athletic ability. It was started in 1977 with a class of eight participants and within two years it grew to include five classes with about sixty to eighty people.

This circuit is based on a time interval of thirty seconds. A tape recorder is used to signal the start of each exercise and the end at ten, fifteen or twenty seconds. Beginners should stop exercising at ten seconds. After they get used to the workouts they can move on to fifteen and eventually twenty seconds of active exercise. A Universal Gym is used as the central piece of equipment and the circuit is organized around it. Barbells and dumbbells are used to complement the exercises available on the gym.

Initially only a twelve-exercise circuit was used. However, we wanted to include more exercises for a more complete workout and, due to the popularity of the program, we needed to be able to handle more people. For these reasons, we started using a six-teen-exercise circuit as the standard. We almost always run the circuit three times, with no rest between circuits.

An even number of exercises are used and the participants start at every other exercise. This allows some pieces of equipment to be used for two different exercises. For example, typically, the bench press station is used for both the bench press and shoulder shrugs. Thus, for a sixteen-exercise circuit, eight people at a time can be accommodated.

At a usual noon workout two sixteen-exercise circuits are run. But when more than sixteen people show up, one is replaced with a shorter circuit (fifteen exercises) that requires no duplicate usage of equipment. You can be very flexible in the numbers of people who work out together as long as you have a good facility. Here are the two standard Boulder Circuits:

12-EXERCISE CIRCUIT

Exercise Number	Exercise	Equipment
1	Sit-ups	Inclined board
2	Wrist curls	Barbell and chair
3	Bench press	Bench press station
4	Shoulder shrugs	Bench press station
5	Leg extension	Leg machine
6	Leg flexion	Leg machine
7	Military press	Military press station

8	Back extension	Extension station
9	Arm curls	Curling station
10	Side bends	Dumbbells
11	Lat pull-downs	High-lat station
12	Leg press	Leg press station

SUPER CIRCUIT

Exercise Number	Exercise	Equipment
1	Sit-ups	Inclined board
2	Wrist curls	Barbell and chair
3	Bench press	Bench press station
4	Shoulder shrugs	Bench press station
5	Leg extension	Leg machine
6	Leg flexion	Leg machine
7	Military press	Military press station
8	Back extension	Extension station
9	Swimmer's kick	Extension station
10	Arm curls	Curling station
11	Side bends	Barbells
12	Leg raises	Inclined board
13	Leg press	Leg press station
14	Calf raise	Leg press station
15	Lat pull-down	High lat station
16	Supine, laterial arm raises (flies)	Barbells and a bench

The order in which exercises are done is determined by the arrangement of equipment in the room and the flow of traffic. The twelve-exercise circuit involves a simple movement, counter-clockwise, around the room (viewed from above). The sixteen-exercise circuit is more complex. In order to separate exercises for the same muscular groups, it contains a counterclockwise revolution within a counterclockwise revolution. Sometimes these do-loops can be terminal; some individuals always get lost. There are two rules to enforce to ensure a good workout. First, anyone who doesn't know where to go next must ask before the end of the exercise, otherwise there is no time to tell them. Second, the person who is out of place must give way to everyone else. Lost souls do jumping jacks until they get reoriented.

The Boulder Circuit has proven to be very popular and a very efficient means of training people. Because the participants can substitute exercises for those in the basic circuit, they can tailor the program to their own needs. For example, most people are encouraged to substitute revised flies for the calf raise. This change achieves a better muscle balance for most participants but does not interfere with the workout of those who follow the established circuit.

THE OCTC CIRCUIT

There are many different parcourses, fitness trails and OCTC's (outdoor circuit training courses). Our favorite is described below.

It is our favorite because it is based on established training principles. Stretching is done before and after the circuit is run. A total of ten stretching exercises are included. The strength exercise stations are constructed to accommodate a variety of strength levels. Also, they are designed to isolate and overload the muscles being exercised.

Running the OCTC once a week and doing aerobic strength training with weights two days a week is recommended. Alternate days should be devoted to long, slow distance work.

The exercises included are:

Exercise Number	Exercise	Equipment
1	Arm circles	None
2	Sit-ups	Inclined boards
3	Push-ups	Elevated pipe
4	Swimmer's kick	Extension station
5	Hop kick*	None
6	Chin-ups	High bars
7	Calf raise	elevated 4" x 4"

*To do hop kicks hold your arms out to your sides. Kick one foot up to the hand on that side. Drop that leg and repeat the kick on the other side. Try to find a rhythm at which you kick one leg, hop, then kick the other.

8	Dips	Parallel bars
9	Step-ups	Steps
10	Ladder walk	Elevated ladder
11	Jumping jacks	None
12	Back extension	Extension station
13	Hip raise	Elevated pipe
14	Leg raises	Inclined board
15	Balance beam	4" x 6" beam

When this course is run more than once in a workout, start at one par level (intensity) below your normal. Also jog through the course, without doing the exercises, between the two runs.

PACE

PACE is the acronym used by European Health Spas to denote their circuit training program. The acronym stands for Personal Aerobic Circuit Exercise.

PACE has a thirty-second exercise period and fifteen-second rest period between sets. Thus, both the exercise period and the rest period are slightly longer than with the Boulder Circuit.

To ensure that the heart rate is elevated to within the training level appropriate for your age, your first exercise is on a stationary bicycle. You pedal for about three minutes or until your pulse is elevated high enough. Then you start on the following circuit:

Exercise Number	Exercise	Equipment
1	Bench press	Bench press station
2	Lat pull down	High lat machine
3	Leg press	Leg press machine
4	Standing press	Military press station
5	Arm curls	Curling machine
6	Leg flexion	Leg machine
7	Upright rows	Curling machine
8	Sit-ups	Inclined board
9	Leg extension	Leg machine

Then it's back to the bicycle. Beginners usually stop after one circuit. As your conditioning improves you can add more circuits, up to three total. Bicycling is done between each circuit. Unfortunately there is little encouragement to substitute exercises or expand the circuit.

OTHER CIRCUITS

Dr. Paul Ward, of the Health and Tennis Corporation of America, has devised a circuit program that encourages the participants to run between exercises. There are ten exercises and each is performed for thirty seconds in each of three circuits. Between each exercise everyone runs for thirty seconds. Exercise weights are selected based on the maximum weight with which a person could do one repetition. The weights used in the circuit program are 40 percent of this maximum.

The exercises are:

Exercise Number	Exercise	Equipment
1	Squat	Barbell
2	Shoulder pass	Barbell
3	Leg curl	Leg machine
4	Arm curl	Curling station
5	Leg Press	Leg press station
6	Bench press	Bench press station
7	Sit-ups	Inclined board
8	Triceps	High lat station
9	Back extension	Extension station
10	Lateral arm raises	Dumbbells

Professor Pat O'Shea, a coach at Oregon State University, recommends doing bursts of strength exercises for forty-five seconds and resting up to a minute between exercises. In his program he has participants do fifteen to twenty repetitions in a forty-five second interval. When a participant can do twenty repetitions of an exercise, he increases the weight. Professor O'Shea arranges the exercises so that there is an alternation between leg, arm, trunk and shoulder exercises. Here are his two recommended circuits:

Exercise Number	Exercise Circuit A	Exercise Circuit B
1	Bench press	Inclined press
2	Squats	Hack squats

3	Bent arm pullover	Leg raise
4	Upright row	Arm curls
5	Dead lift	Dips
6	Lat pull down	Standing lateral raise
7	Sit-up	Bent rows
8	Curl	Power snatch

(These programs are described in O'Shea's book *Scientific Principle and Methods of Strength Fitness*. Hack squat is a squat, but the bar is held behind the legs instead of on the back of the shoulders. Heels are elevated on a board for better stability. The snatch is a competitive lift that we do not suggest for fitness training.

Scientists at the Institute for Aerobics Research have conducted several studies on aerobic strength training. In one program they adjusted the weights used to 50 percent of the 1 RM, which is the maximum weight lifted at one repetition. They retested every two weeks and adjusted the weights accordingly. The participants did two circuits of the exercise. Inititally, they rested thirty seconds between sets of exercises. Later, the resting interval was reduced to twenty-five seconds and finally to twenty seconds. They attempted to do fifteen repetitions of each exercise in each set.

The ten exercises in the circuit are:

Exercise Number	Exercise	Equipment
1	Bench press	Bench press station
2	Leg extension	Leg machine
3	Leg flexion	Leg machine
4	Arm curls	Barbell
5	Dips	Dipping station
6	Leg press	Leg press station
7	Sit-ups	Inclined board
8	Shoulder press	Military press station
9	Lat pull down	High lat station
10	Upright rows	Curling station

YOUR OWN PROGRAM

Examples of aerobic strength training programs for general fitness have been presented. You can pick one of these or create your own program. To date, research has not indicated that one method is to be preferred over the others, so you should use whatever system you like best.

You might try changing the timing sequence and the selection of exercises every six weeks. When you continue with the same training program for a long time your body adapts to it but might not continue to improve. Also it is fun to experiment and to see how you react to different exercise stress.

The particular program used is much less important than your consistency and determination in training, that is, as long as you follow the established training principles for cardiovascular and strength training. Locate a good facility, join a friendly group to train with and hold yourself to your schedule and you will see your condition improve.

HOW MUCH FITNESS IS FIT ENOUGH?

Like many activities in life, the pursuit of fitness follows a law of diminishing returns. People who are in the worst condition can gain the most when they increase their exercise activity. Someone who is running seventy miles a week will get very little, if any, fitness benefit by increasing his mileage by ten miles a week. However, someone who never runs would benefit greatly if he started to run ten miles a week.

This is the concept I presented in the *Complete Circuit Training Guide,* and have reproduced, in part, here. A fitness curve has been drawn and units of exercise, in terms of miles a week run, have been annotated on the horizontal axis. A qualitative scale of conditioning is represented on the vertical scale (see next page).

As the number of miles run increases, to the right of the scale, the level of conditioning increases, upward on the scale. We have divided the fitness curve into three phases. These divisions are somewhat arbitrary but can serve as at least a semi-quantitive guide for progress in a future program of running and indoor circuit training. Outdoor circuit training is equally applicable but much harder to quantify by this method. Here are the fitness phases and our suggested corresponding workout program.

Phase I. Not presently participating in any regular exercise program. Map out a course that you think you can comfortably walk and run. You may need to start with a distance as short as one-half mile. Your initial objective should be to complete the course without discomfort, while alternately walking and running. Incrementally increase the length of your course to about two miles. Then gradually increase the percentage of the distance that you run. The ultimate goal of Phase I is to be able to cover a two-mile course in less than twenty-four minutes, at least five days a week.

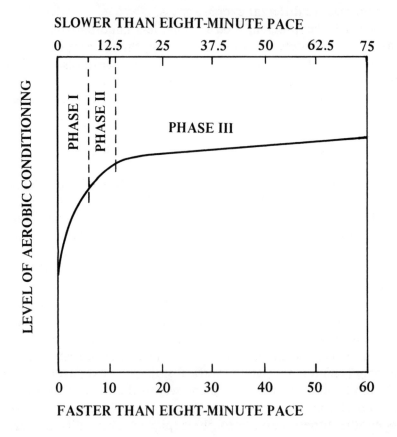

Phase II. Being able to pass one of Cooper's aerobics tests—covering 1.5 miles in less than twelve minutes or being able to score above fifty on the Harvard Step Test. Start indoor or outdoor aerobic strength training at a pace that is comfortable for you. These workouts should be conducted three days a week. Continue your walking/running program on alternate days. Try swimming or cycling in place of jogging. If you prefer either of these to running, use it as the focus of your training program. Gradually increase the distance that you run, swim, or cycle, and gradually increase the duration of the exercise cycle in indoor aerobic strength training.

Phase III. Being able to do three strenuously paced circuits at maximum duration (for example, at 20-10). Use more weight for those exercises that have become too easy. Consider adding additional exercises to the circuit. Increase the distance of your running, swimming, or cycling, and consider increasing the speed. Use an outdoor circuit training course alternatively with indoor training and try to reduce your elapsed time. Increase your par or the number of repetitions on your OCTC circuit. Add a short run or some other aerobic exercise after doing aerobic strength training.

When you are in Phase III you are treating your body to a strenuous, well-rounded fitness program. Beyond this level of training, improvements in fitness come slowly and probably cannot be justified on a purely physical fitness basis. Increasing the intensity or frequency of workouts should be done for added enjoyment or in preparation for competition.

A good place to stop expanding your training efforts is somewhere in Phase III, where the curve starts to approach a horizontal line. In Phases I and II the conditioning benefits certainly warrant the increased level of training. But beyond the start of Phase III you see little improvement. This is not to say that you should stop there. If you work out because you are training for competition or because you enjoy the workouts, then certainly continue. But if you must drag yourself through a workout to stay fit you might be overtraining.

Our point is that there is a level of optimum fitness, defined in terms of time and effort invested versus benefits achieved. That level, which must be determined by each individual, is located in the region where the fitness curve approaches a horizontal line. This curve applies only to aerobic conditioning, but if you have a total exercise program—that is, one that includes flexibility and strength training—you will be developing all the elements of fitness along with aerobic conditioning.

Also, be aware that overtraining can, and does occur. Once you are in Phase III, you will find a maximum sustainable effort in your training program. There are optimum levels of training, beyond which fatigue and injuries become more common. Thus, although the fitness curve shows an ever-increasing benefit for additional training, in reality each person has some practical upper limit.

9

Sports

Aerobic strength training is an ideal training technique for many sports because it is so versatile. The strength and cardiovascular needs for each sport are different but aerobic strength training programs can be designed to simulate the conditions of the sport. The programs discussed in Chapter 8, General Fitness, are useful as general conditioning programs for any sport. However, you can modify these to nearly duplicate in training the conditions you will encounter in your sport.

We have had experience in training people with interests in a variety of sports: running, skiing, swimming, gymnastics, dancing and bicycling. Also, we have prescribed exercise routines for a variety of other sports.

In recommending a training program we analyze the strength, endurance and cardiovascular requirements of the sport. The strength requirements of most sports can be analyzed quickly. By watching the movements of a sport you can learn which principle muscle groups are involved. Antagonistic muscle groups, those that oppose the action of principle muscle groups, must also be included in a training schedule. Other muscles that do not directly contribute to the movement in a sport can be included if the athlete has a history of injury or weakness. For example, a cyclist may always get sore muscles in the back of his neck, especially early in the season. Neck extension exercises would be included to strengthen these muscles. By eliminating the problem of sore neck muscles, the athlete can train harder and better.

After the muscles to be exercised have been identified, you must decide what type of work to give them. For most sports the

159

goal of strength training is to develop strong muscles that can repeat a motion over and over. Training should take a similar form.
You should also consider the specifics of the movements you are
hoping to strengthen. During the pre-season training period, the
motions exercised in the weight room should duplicate as closely
as possible the specific motions of the sport.

The timing of each exercise, each set, or each circuit, and the
entire workout, can be modified to meet your needs. The general
fitness circuits, recommended in the previous chapters, are a good
place to start. However, after you have become accustomed to
aerobic strength training, you can experiment by changing the
timing sequence.

You should train in the same way you play. In tennis, for example, you have a brief rest between each point and between each
set. Your training can reflect this. Decide what the longest con-
ceivable volley would be and use this as the time for one set. Di-
vide the time up into a series of twenty- or thirty-second intervals
in which you will exercise. Because you may not get all of your
exercises in one set, you could have two or more sets of different
exercises. Rest for thirty seconds between sets but work out until
you have completed three full sets of each exercise.

Obviously, this type of workout will have a strong anaerobic
component. Although we call our system Aerobic Strength Training, it is equally applicable to anaerobic conditioning. Match the
workout design to your sport and you will develop the cardiovascular conditioning you need, whether it is aerobic, anaerobic, or
more likely, a combination.

Much of the information needed to design an exercise plan is
available from coaches and books. You can transform this information from recommendations for conventional training programs
to an outline for an aerobic strength training program.

Training for sports has become a year-round avocation. No
longer can you be really competitive in a sport if you start training only a few weeks before the first competition. You need to
build the strength and cardiovascular base required for your sport
in the so-called off-season. This phase of the annual training cycle
is when you should isolate muscles to build strength efficiently.
During the pre-season, when you start to practice and refine the
skills of your sport, you need to do exercises that closely mimic
the motions and the speed of movement involved in your sport.
The cardiovascular- and strength-base developed in the off-season

is now applied to your sport. The emphasis in the pre-season should not be to build a basic level of fitness; that should already be done. It should be aimed toward skills training.

During the competitive season, you will have limited time and energy for basic aerobic or strength training. If possible, it is good to continue following your workout schedule at least once a week to maintain your levels of strength and endurance. Even if you cannot keep up the training, your workouts and competition will maintain the strength and cardiovascular levels needed for your sport. It takes a long time and many workouts to build a solid base—it also takes a long time for that base to erode through lack of training. A strong off-season training program can help you have a more enjoyable, competitive and safe sports season.

We will recommended training programs for a variety of sports. For some sports slightly different programs are suggested for the off-season and pre-season. Use these recommendations as a starting point. Then modify the programs in terms of exercise content and training to meet your personal needs.

ALPINE SKIING

Alpine or downhill skiing requires good muscle strength and some degree of cardiovascular fitness. The muscle strength is important in protecting joints and in giving good control. Injuries often occur from falls when muscles tire late in the day. This is especially troublesome for people who ski infrequently. Preparing for the slopes with aerobic strength training can help prevent these injuries.

The most important exercises are those for the quadriceps muscles. Hopping with your knees bent is a great exercise to strengthen them. Other good exercises are stair climbing and squats or leg presses. For aerobic strength training in a gym, use the following exercises in the 15- to 20-repetition range.

Exercise Number	Exercise	Equipment
1	Leg extension	Leg machine
2	Swimmer's kick	Ankle weights
3	Leg raises	Incline board
4	Lateral leg raise	Ankle weights
5	Leg adduction	A partner
6	Back extension	Extension station

7	Sit-ups	None
8	Bent rows	Barbell
9	Triceps press	High lat station

After the workout you should do a series of exercises for the muscles that move the foot at the ankle. Include calf raises, shin strengtheners, and ankle eversion and inversion (outward and inward rotation).

BACKPACKING

Backpacking is obviously not a competitive sport, but it is an outdoor activity that can be safer and more enjoyable if you train for it. You need strength in your leg muscles, both to get you up the hills and to protect your knees and ankles, and in your shoulders and back muscles to carry the load of a backpack. You also need good cardiovascular conditioning, especially if you will be climbing at high elevations.

Do three ankle exercises before or after your aerobic strength workout. These exercises are not well-suited for a high-level cardiovascular workout.

The ankle exercises serve these purposes:

> Ankle eversion - to prevent ankle sprains
> Ankle flexion - to prevent shin splints
> Ankle extension - to push you up the mountain

For your aerobic workout, use either a thirty-second or forty-five-second base—that is, exercise up to twenty seconds or thirty seconds, with the remaining time used for moving to the next station. Between circuits use a stationary bicycle, if one is available. Run an outdoor circuit training course once a week and supplement your aerobic strength workouts with long runs or bike rides, especially on hills.

Exercise Number	Exercise	Equipment
1	Leg extension	Leg machine
2	Leg flexion	Leg machine
3	Sit-ups	None
4	Back extension	Extension station
5	Shoulder shrugs	Bench press station

6	Standing press	Military press station
7	Lat pull down	High lat station
8	Double leg raises	Incline board
9	Swimmer's kick	Extension station

BASEBALL

Aerobic strength training should be used in the off-season to develop explosive strength and some stamina. Start off by working in the eight- to twelve-repetition range, using a thirty-second base. Then, after six to twelve weeks, reduce the repetitions to five to eight. Try resting thirty seconds between circuits.

Exercise Number	Exercises	Equipment
1	Leg extensions	Leg machine
2	Leg flexion	Leg machine
3	Sit-ups	Incline board
4	Arm curls	Dumbbells
5	Bench press	Barbells
6	Standing press	Military press station
7	Lat pulldown	High lat station

There are four other strength building exercises to do: ankle eversion, wrist curls, reverse wrist curls and isometric grip.

BASKETBALL

Basketball requires overall muscle strength and top aerobic conditioning. In the off-season, use a thirty-second base for aerobic training and set the weights so you can do eight to twelve repetitions. During the pre-season increase the repetitions to fifteen to twenty and lengthen the exercise duration to forty-five seconds. During the competitive season you could use a once-a-week maintenance program, but you would probably loose little conditioning if you stopped these programs altogether.

Exercise Number	Exercise	Equipment
1	Leg extension	Leg machine
2	Leg flexion	Leg machine
3	Sit-ups	None

4	Back extension	Extension station
5	Standing press	Military press station
6	Lateral raises	Dumbbells
7	Lat pull downs	High lat station
8	Shoulder shrugs	Bench press station
9	Calf raise	Leg press station
10	Ankle roll overs	None
11	Wrist curls	Barbell
12	Reverse wrist curls	Barbell

In this program wrist curls and ankle roll overs have been included to extend the total duration of the aerobic workout. You may also add or substitute upright rows. Use outdoor circuit training courses once a week.

CANOEING AND KAYAKING

It is difficult to recommend a specific timing sequence for these sports, since the duration of competitive events varies greatly. In training for specific events try to gear either the duration of one circuit or an entire workout to the approximate time your event will last. During the off-season do eight to twelve repetitions in a thirty-second cycle. As the season approaches change to a forty-five-second cycle and increase the repetitions to fifteen to twenty. If isokinetic equipment is available, use it for the arm exercises.

Ideally, you should train the leg muscles isometrically. Your legs either press on foot braces or they support you as you kneel. Also, you hold yourself in the vessel with isometric contractions of your leg abductors or adductors. However, you can build isometric strength adequately with isotonic exercises and the latter lend themselves to aerobic strength programs while the former do not.

Exercise Number	Exercise	Equipment
1	Leg extension	Leg press station
2	Lateral leg raise	Ankle weights
3	Back extension	Extension station
4	Sit-ups	None
5	Supine, alternating arm press	Dumbbells, bench

6	Alternating arm curls	Dumbbells
7	Bent rows	Barbell
8	Lateral arm raise	Dumbbells
9	Lat pull down	High lat machine

CYCLING

There are two reasons to use aerobic strength training for cycling. First, if you cannot train on the roads you can still build strength and endurance in the primary cycling muscles by using the weight room. This training will give you the strength to take best advantage of your training rides as soon as you can get started. The second reason is to build strength in muscles other than the primary muscles. Because these other muscles may not get overload training while cycling, they may not efficiently develop the strength needed for long rides.

Build strength early in the off-season with a thirty-second program, doing eight to twelve repetitions. Increase the repetitions later to at least fifteen to twenty.

Here are two sets of exercises. Do the first when you are not cycling. When you are cycling, do the second.

PROGRAM 1

Exercise Number	Exercise	Equipment
1	Leg extension	Leg machine
2	Leg curls	Leg machine
3	Sit-ups	None
4	Back extension	Extension station
5	Bench press	Bench press station
6	Bent row	Barbell
7	Calf raises	Leg press station
8	Leg press	Leg press station
9	Ankle flexion (toe raise)	Ankle weights
10	Neck extension	Head harness or neck machine

PROGRAM 2

Exercise Number	Exercise	Equipment
1	Back extension	Extension station
2	Sit-ups	None
3	Push-ups	None
4	Bent rows	Barbell
5	Standing press	Military press station
6	Lat pull downs	High lat station
7	Wrist curls	Barbell
8	Reverse wrist curls	Barbell

GOLF

Golf is not an aerobic sport but does rely on good muscle tone. We present an aerobic strength training regime for golf as a combined program of aerobics for general cardiovascular fitness and muscle tone. Do eight to twelve repetitions. Also do isometric grip exercises. Use a cylindrical object about the same diameter as your club shaft, or use your clubs for the grip exercises.

Exercise Number	Exercise	Equipment
1	Squats	Barbell
2	Back extension	Extension station
3	Sit-ups	None
4	Bench press	Bench press station
5	Arm curl	Barbell
6	Arm lateral raise	Dumbbells
7	Wrist curl	Barbell
8	Reverse wrist curl	Barbell

GYMNASTICS

Gymnastics is a term that describes a collection of exercises or events. Strength requirements in each event are different. The following program is a general aerobic strength program. Gymnasts who need help for specific events should substitute appropriate exercises.

In this program you should do eight to twelve repetitions in a thirty-second cycle. Rest thirty seconds between the three circuits.

Exercise Number	Exercise	Equipment
1	Leg extension	Leg press station
2	Double leg raise	Incline board
3	Back extension	Extension station
4	Sit-ups	None
5	Dips	Parallel bars
6	Arm curls	Dumbbells
7	Standing press	Barbell
8	Lat pull downs	High lat station
9	Calf raise	Leg press

MARTIAL ARTS

For competition, arrange your training so it matches the duration of a round. Use eight to twelve repetitions in three circuits and thirty seconds for each set. The number of exercises suggested is more than you should use in one circuit. You could do some of the exercises after your aerobic workout—neck flexion and extension, grip, wrist flexion and extension and ankle roll overs. For your aerobic workout use the following exercises:

Exercise Number	Exercise	Equipment
1	Squats	Barbell
2	Swimmer's kick	Extension station
3	Double leg raise	Incline board
4	Back extension	Extension station
5	Sit-ups	Incline board
6	Upright rows	Curling station
7	Lat pull down	High lat station

NORDIC SKIING

For cross-country skiing, start early in the off-season by building strength. Use eight to twelve repetitions. When you have established a good base of strength, reduce the weights so you can do twenty to thirty repetitions in a forty-five-second circuit.

During the strength-building phase, use only exercises that will isolate your muscles. In the latter stages you can add exercises that more closely mimic the particular motions involved in cross-country skiing.

After your aerobic strength workout, do the following exercises: ankle eversion (ankle roll overs), ankle inversion, ankle flexion (skin strengtheners) and leg abductors. Do six to ten repetitions on the last two exercises but on the others do twenty to thirty.

Exercise Number	Exercise	Equipment
1	Leg extension	Leg machine
2	Leg flexion	Leg machine
3	Swimmer's kick	Extension station
4	Back extension	Extension station
5	Double leg raise	Incline board
6	Sit-ups	Incline board
7	Triceps press	High lat station
8	Bent lateral raise	Dumbbells
9	Lateral arm raise	Dumbbells
10	Lat pull down	High lat station

In the pre-season, substitute the following four exercises. Do an alternating arm swing with dumbbells. Be sure that you use a weight heavy enough so that you reach muscle fatigue. Another arm-swing exercise is done while lying face down on a bench. Hold a dumbbell in each hand and swing it forward and to the rear, close along the bench.

Replace lateral arm raises with a similar exercise performed while you are lying face down on a bench. Holding a dumbbell in each arm, swing the dumbbells first toward your head and then back to your sides.

You can replace both the leg extension and swimmer's kick exercises with one exercise at the leg press station. Face the opposite direction you would for doing leg presses. Rest one knee on the seat with your thigh along the seat back. Place your other foot on the pedal of the leg press. Push the pedals forward with that foot.

RACKET SPORTS

Racket sports require fast muscle contractions and overall strength, your training program should reflect this. Do exercises for a variety of muscles and do each repetition explosively. Use a forty-five-second time base and try to do fifteen repetitions in that time.

Exercise Number	Exercise	Equipment
1	Squats	Barbell
2	Leg curls	Leg machine
3	Back extension	Extension station
4	Sit-ups	None
5	Wide-grip bench press	Bench press station
6	Reverse arm curls	Barbell
7	Bent lateral raise	Dumbbells
8	Supine lateral raise	Dumbbells
9	Lateral arm raise	Dumbbells
10	Lat pull down	High lat station

After the workout do three sets of the following exercises at fifteen to twenty repetitions each, calf raise, ankle roll overs, wrist curls and reverse wrist curls, and isometric grip exercises.

RUNNING

Although sprinters have frequented weight rooms for some time, middle- and long-distance runners generally have not. However, more and more runners are finding that strength training can be compatible with and even beneficial for running.

Improvements in strength fitness can restrict the possibilities of injury by stabilizing joints susceptible to overuse injuries and by helping balance opposing muscle groups. They can also build the strength needed for long runs, both in the primary driving muscles in the legs and in the upper body muscles that often do not get training through progressive overloading.

Most runners will not notice a significant increase in muscle bulk. However, if an undesirable increase occurs, the runner need only eliminate the exercises that contributed to it or reduce the overall strength training program. The muscles will get smaller, or atrophy, with reduced use.

SPRINTS

Sprints are anaerobic and strength training for sprints also should be anaerobic. To develop anaerobic capacity while strength training use a timed sequence of equal periods of exercise and rest. For short sprints use fifteen seconds. For long sprints use thirty seconds—that is, thirty seconds of rapid exercising followed by thirty seconds of recovery. Do each repetition as fast as possible to develop explosive power.

Exercise Number	Exercise	Equipment
1	Leg press	Leg press station
2	Leg curls	Leg machine
3	Swimmer's kick	Ankle weights
4	Double leg raises	Incline board
5	Back extension	Extension station
6	Dips	Dipping station
7	Arm curls	Barbell
8	Bent alternating rows	Dumbbells
9	Standing press	Military press station
10	Lat pull down	High lat station

Also do calf raises at a leg press station and shin strengtheners with ankle weights around your toes.

DISTANCE RUNNING

If you are not running in the off-season, add leg extensions and curls and double leg raises to the following list. During the pre-season add dumbbell arm swings, which mimic arm movement during running. To do this exercise hold a pair of light dumbbells as if you were at a dipping station. Swing one forward and the other to the rear as far as possible. Also do ankle rollovers and shin strengtheners after your aerobic strength workout.

Use a thirty-second base and work toward doing fifteen repetitions in each set. Do your aerobic strength workouts on days when you have scheduled a light run.

Exercise Number	Exercise	Equipment
1	Swimmer's kick	Extension station
2	Back extension	Extension station
3	Sit-ups	None
4	Bent rows	Barbell
5	Wide-grip bench press	Bench press station
6	Upright row	Rowing station
7	Standing press	Military press station
8	Lat pull down	High lat station

Add as many as eight other exercises to extend the workout. Try bicycling or running between circuits. Use an outdoor circuit training course if one is available or make your own around a track.

SNOWSHOEING

Snowshoeing is a demanding sport, whether you engage in it for competition or for outdoor pleasure. Part of the demand, or the aches and pains, of snowshoeing comes from needing strength in several muscle groups that often get little exercise. These groups are the leg abductors, hip flexors, and ankle flexors (shin muscles). Other important muscles are the calf muscles and the quadriceps muscles in the thigh.

Since most practitioners of the sport do it only on weekends you can continue your training program throughout the season. Do fifteen repetitions in a thirty-second base circuit.

Exercise Number	Exercise	Equipment
1	Squats	Barbell
2	Double leg raise	Incline board
3	Lateral leg raise	Incline board
4	Back extension	Extension station
5	Swimmer's kick	Ankle weights

6	Sit-ups	None
7	Calf raises	Leg press station
8	Toe raises	Ankle weights

If you use ski poles, add the triceps press and bent alternating rows with dumbbells.

SOCCER

Aerobic strength training is especially applicable to off-season training in soccer. Use a forty-five-second circuit and do fifteen to twenty repetitions in the thirty-second active phase. Interspace jumping jacks, running in place with high knee action or cycling on a stationary bicycle.

Exercise Number	Exercise	Equipment
1	Leg extension	Leg machine
2	Leg curls	Leg machine
3	Lateral leg raise	Incline board
4	Leg adduction	None - a partner is required
5	Back extension	Extension station
6	Sit-ups	None
7	Bent rows	Barbell
8	Standing press	Military press station

After your aerobic strength workout do one set of the following exercises, ankle flexion (skin strengtheners), ankle roll overs, neck extension and neck flexion.

SWIMMING

More and more swimming coaches are recommending out-of-the-pool strength training for their swimmers. Doc Counselman recommends it but warns that swimmers should refrain from muscle building exercises for muscles that do not directly contribute to propulsion through the water. He is concerned with swimmers gaining muscle bulk in muscles that do not help win races; the added bulk will slow swimmers down.

In the off-season build strength by using a thirty-second base circuit and staying in the eight- to twelve-repetition range. If iso-kinetics equipment is available, switch to it later in your training schedule and use a timing sequence that coincides with the duration of your event.

Exercise Number	Exercise	Equipment
1	Leg extension	Leg machine (isotonic or isokinetic)
2	Swimmer's kick	Ankle weights
3	Triceps press	High lat station or mini-gym
4	Supine lateral raises (flies)	Dumbbells
5	Lat pull down	High lat station or mini-gym
6	Calf raise	Leg press station
7	Double leg raise	Incline board
8	Back extension	Extension station
9	Sit-ups	None

VOLLEYBALL

Volleyball requires good leaping ability, coordination and strength. Aerobic condition has only secondary importance, but is benefical in developing stamina for long tournament play. Do twelve to fifteen repetitions of the following exercises in an aerobic strength circuit.

Exercise Number	Exercise	Equipment
1	Squats	Barbell
2	Hamstring curls	Leg machine
3	Back extension	Extension station
4	Abdominal curls	None
5	Military press	Barbell
6	Straight arm pulldown	High lat station
7	Calf raise	Leg press station
8	Ankle roll overs	None
9	Wrist curls	Barbell

WRESTLING

Use this program in the off-season. When wrestling workouts start, you will probably need to discontinue it or reduce it to one workout per week. Train in the eight- to twelve-repetition range in a thirty-second circuit. Rest one minute between circuits. Also do one set of each of the following exercises—neck extension and flexion, wrist curls and reverse wrist curls and back extension.

Exercise Number	Exercise	Equipment
1	Squat	Barbell
2	Swimmer's kick	Ankle weights
3	Sit-ups	None
4	Dips	Dipping station
5	Chin ups	Chinning bar
6	Bent rows	Barbell
7	Standing press	Military press station

10

Keys to Success

The first key to success is to apply the accepted principles of training in your workouts. Many people go through the motions of exercising without getting anywhere. The efforts they expend probably do not net them the results they want. The problem is that they are not working smartly. A good example of this is when people strength train without overloading their muscles. As shown in Chapter 3, muscle gains while underloaded are very slow. Another example is training above or below the cardiovascular training limits. You could put in a lot of miles without greatly improving your aerobic conditioning. The last example is the use of a valid training principle to develop conditioning that is not useful in the sport the person is training for.

Here are the accepted principles. First, stretch your muscles to make them as flexible as possible. Some people need more stretching than others, and some people can stretch farther than others. Be concerned only with your own stretching program and follow it day in and out.

Second, in cardiovascular training, work within your training limits. Refer to the table in Chapter 2 to get what the limits are for your age.

Third, to build strength, isolate the muscles, progressively overload them, work them to muscle fatigue, and repeat the sets and the workout over a long period. Doing complex motions involves many muscles, only one of which may get overloaded in an exercise. By doing simple, isolated exercises, you can work each muscle or muscle group to its limit, thus helping it get stronger. The greatest failure in strength training is that people quit when the muscles just start to tire. This is when strength is built. The first few repetitions, the ones everyone does, don't do anything except prepare the muscle for the important last few repetitions. Always try for one more rep. After you have completed one set of an exercise, repeat the set. Repeat the workout two days later and again two days after that. Consistent repetition is essential. Also, it should be obvious that each repetition must be done with correct form.

Between workouts get adequate rest and a well balanced diet. To grow, the muscles need protein, but not outrageously high intakes of protein.

The specificity principle is a final important point. You should train the specific muscles, in the specific motions, at the specific speeds you will use in your sport. Pushing football tackling dummies is not the best program for a ballet dancer. The cardiovascular part of your training should be as carefully matched to the requirements of your sport as are the strength aspects.

In sports, the winner is the person who best performs a specialized task, not the person who can perform many different tasks fairly well. Design your training program so it will help you, and eliminate all extraneous elements. This will allow you to concentrate your energies where they are needed.

The second key to success is to find a training regime that is comfortable for you. If you must drive fifty miles to get to the facility, and you hate to drive, you probably won't go. If you dislike the atmosphere, equipment, locker rooms or anything else about a facility, you will soon discontinue your program.

Also, the program must be comfortable. If you hate it or if you don't feel you are getting the results you want, you will soon quit. Don't be afraid to change programs. You should do so often. Check your progress and modify the program accordingly.

Although this key to success is valid for any training, it is especially useful for aerobic srength training. That is because aeorbic strength training is so versatile. You can modify a program to meet your needs, that is, to make it more comfortable for you.

Part of establishing a comfortable program is building a group, the members of which share your dedication. Few of us have the drive to carry on a top-flight training program alone. But with a small group it is much easier. Your partners in training make it easier to work out on a regular basis. After all, they are waiting for you at the gym at an established time. They can help in more direct ways, like criticizing your form and setting weights and spotting you on barbell exercises. They also can make workouts more fun.

We recommend coed groups. There is absolutely no reason not to and many people will enjoy the workouts much more.

Another part of being comfortable with your exercise program is continuing your existing workouts. If you have been running for years, don't give it up when you take up aerobic strength training. Blend the two parts of your program together.

The third key to success is to keep at it. Progress is not achieved in a few workouts. Improvements in conditioning occur over a long period with consistent workouts. While others are debating the fastest ways to train, you can be improving steadily by continuing your workouts. One way to help you be consistent was mentioned above—work with a group. Another way is to keep records of your workouts or at least of the results of periodic retesting. These will show how you have improved and where you need more work. They are an ideal place to write down your goals. Later compare results with goals and try to understand any significant differences between them.

These are the three general keys to success:

- use the proven principles in your workouts
- find and use a program that is comfortable
- stick with your program.

You can reach your training goals through the intelligent application of these keys. Happy circuit training.

About the Authors

Ed Sobey is the director of the Science Museum and Planetarium of Palm Beach County, Inc., in West Palm Beach, Florida. Previously, Ed taught aerobic strength training at the Boulder, Colorado, YMCA and founded a sports program for the blind in Boulder. He has written three books on fitness and a variety of magazine articles. He has a Ph.D. in oceanography and has participated in or lead expeditions to the Antarctic, Alaska, South America, and across the Pacific in a sailboat. In addition to his interest in running and strength training, Sobey pursues diving, canoeing, kayaking and skiing.

Gary Burns is the assistant sports editor at the *Daily Camera* newspaper in Boulder, Colorado, where he has worked the past four years. He graduated from the University of Colorado in 1974 with a bachelor's degree in journalism, and was a Boettcher Foundation Scholar. Burns lives in Louisville, Colorado. His interests include running, racquetball and photography.

Recommended Reading

The following books, also available from Anderson World, can augment your exercise and fitness program. They are available from major bookstores or can be ordered directly from the publisher (1400 Stierlin Road, Mountain View, CA 94043).

THE RUNNER'S WORLD YOGA BOOK by Jean Couch with Nell Weaver. An easy-to-follow guide to using the principles of yoga for stretching, strengthening, and toning the body, and a good book to graduate to after making the initial commitment to embark on a fitness and health program. Spiral bound. $11.95; pbk. $9.95.

THE RUNNER'S WORLD INDOOR EXERCISE BOOK by Richard Benyo and Rhonda Provost. A simple-to-understand guide to fitness and the exercising body, and how it responds to beginning exercise programs, with programs keyed to the beginner and oriented toward getting started comfortably indoors before moving into outdoor fitness training and outdoor sports. Spiral bound. $11.95; pbk. $9.95.

THE RUNNER'S WORLD NATURAL FOODS COOKBOOK by Pamela Hannan. An easy-to-follow guide to recipes without sugar, with special attention to the vitamins that can be received from properly prepared food. Extensive recipes in a variety of categories. Spiral bound. $11.95.

THE RUNNER'S WORLD WEIGHT CONTROL BOOK by Michael Nash. A logical, realistic approach to losing weight and keeping it off forever that ignores the fad diets and gets right to the root of the problem: one's own image of self. A complete course in getting away from the multi-course meal. Spiral bound. $11.95; pbk. $9.95.

DANCE AEROBICS by Maxine Polley. The rage that has swept the nation. Getting in shape and staying there through an ambitious program of enjoyable, fast-moving dance that builds aerobic fitness while toning muscles and doing away with unwanted weight. Quality paperback. $5.95.

GETTING YOUR EXECUTIVES FIT by Don T. Jacobs, Ph.D. The book that America's corporations have been waiting for. A book that, in one package, reviews all available information on corporate fitness, while making the information accessible to everyone from hourly worker to chairman of the board. Large format paperback. $12.95.